ACKNOWLEDGEMENT

THANK YOU HAROLD!

WITHOUT YOU, THIS BOOK

WOULD ABSOLUTELY NOT EXIST!

- Constance Williams Watson

DEDICATION

TO GIRLS OF EVERY COLOR FOUND UNDER THE SUN.

TO GIRLS OF EVERY AGE…..0 to 125.

TO GIRLS WHO LIVE EVERY PLACE UNDER THE SKY.

- Constance Williams Watson

Table Of Conents

Introduction

I have joyfully spent the last thirty years of my life serving and walking alongside females of various ages. I love being female. I love interacting with females. I greatly value and respect females. In my opinion, females are the glue that holds our daily lives, our families and our world together.

I believe there is a shared role that most females around the world share. It is taking care of our children and taking care of our family members. Sharing this common role in life, females around the world have an understanding of each other's emotions, struggles, concerns, and "matters of the heart," without the need for spoken words. I would describe this as a bond. For me, there is an unseen bond that ties my heart to other females without knowing them. Haven't you felt that connection when you watched the mother on TV holding her baby who is dying from starvation or thirst and is helpless to save her baby?

To me, the irreplaceability of females in our world is evident. Look around you. What do you think would happen to our families, schools, hospitals, daycare centers, churches, senior/elder care

My point is that females hold the most important things in life together, so females deserve to have the best life possible. My thirty years of serving females and my story here in this book are my contributions to you having your best life possible because I know you deserve it. Hopefully, I will be able to do more in the future.

I have tagged all females as "girls" for this book. I even chose to order myself a "girl," and here's why I say this. The first reason is that we might recognize the value and the beauty in each other without any age barriers. I want to be inclusive. My age range for girls is 0 to 120 years old. Hopefully, that will include all of us. Even the little unborn girls still tucked inside their Moms are included.

The second reason for calling all of us "girls" is that no matter how old we may be, there is still a little girl deep down inside us. That is why many eighty-five-year-old girls continue to paint their nails red or bright pink and are never seen in public without their lipstick or at least lip-gloss. Every girl likes to look pretty. I am like her. I may not be young anymore, but I am still a little girl on the inside.

The third reason is that many of us, especially African-Americans, already address each other as "girls," signifying a common female bond and sisterhood. My daughter and I often call each other girl. Sometimes it's ggirrrlll, depending on what's gone down.

And fourth, by calling us all girls, there might be a simple and more unified assembling of multi-generational females, where the young girls and the elder-age girls sit at the table together and tell their stories and glean from another's account. My daughter and I are working together on a project we hope will bring many more opportunities for gatherings like that.

His Girl! is my story, and my story is the platform I have been given to contribute to making every girl's life the best it can be. My story is about the sweet rain and the bitter rain that have fallen on my life and the life of my family. If you are in a family, there will be some sweet rain days, as well as some bitter rain days for you, too. My story is about my life from a girl of about age five to the seventy-two-year-old girl I am today, more specifically about the more than forty years of my life when I did not know I was God's girl! How is the little girl inside you doing?

I hope that it will be helpful to every girl who takes the spiritual journey with me. As I tell my story, you will notice no names are given to my family members. Instead of using false names, I have chosen to identify some people I speak about using the name of a type of fabric I think matches the person's personality.

One of my favorite "girl things" to do has been to go on an all-girl road trip. You too, huh? If I got a call from a couple of my close girlfriends who are still good drivers right now wanting to take a fun road trip, I would try to make it happen. In my younger days, I was also known for going on the road alone. My daughter would not stand for that today, even though I am still a good driver.

I especially enjoyed driving from my home here in Atlanta, GA, back to my hometown in Morganton, NC. But if given a choice, I would choose an all-girl road trip any day. Either way, I never left home for a long drive without my *Frankie Beverly and Maze* CD. I fell for his music and his songs back in the 1970s.

As you begin reading this book, I would like for you to imagine or pretend, as little girls do, that you and I have just loaded up in my 2002 Toyota Sienna mini-van (I heard that) for a road trip back into my past, and that we are on our way. As we pull off, I will slip in my Frankie Beverly CD and find my favorite song, *"Joy and Pain, Sunshine and Rain."* I loved the beat for dancing and the words because they spoke the real truth about real life. Life is composed of joy and pain, which I and many others call sunshine and rain.

But I like the rain. Without rain, people, plants, and animal life could not survive. The rain came in two forms in my life: there has been bitter rain and sweet rain. In the end, it took both the bitter rain and the sweet rain to get me to where *HE* was taking me.

When your road trip with me is over, my greatest desire is that you would know that you belong to Him – the God in you! I want you to see and know that you are *His Girl* too. Even if you haven't chosen Him yet or may feel you never will, He has plans to win you over so you can fulfill the purpose for which He created you. Whether you were 6 or 106 when you chose Him, once you do, you will be His forever no matter what.

Although I walked away from Him at eight-years-old and spent the next thirty-two years of my life rejecting Him, I found out I was still *His Girl*. I chose to leave Him and walk away, but He never rejected or walked away from me. When I first decided on Him at six-years-old, I became His for life -- I became His Girl!! Life is a journey, a road trip with God. Your journey, like mine, will bring some joy and some pain, some sunshine and some rain, but you will get to where *HE* is taking you because no matter what your life brings, **You can be His Girl!** Let the road trip begin!!

Chapter 1

Sunshine, Tadpoles and Family

I am positive that Labor Day, September 4, 1948, had to be a day my mother and her closest girlfriends would always remember, not because it was my birthday, but because I came into this world weighing 10lbs. 4oz.! My mother gave birth to me in the "Colored Ward" at the hospital, where I am sure she did not get the princess treatment, and she endured all of it without the help of an epidural. This is the stuff nightmares are made of for today's women. For her, it was Labor Day for real, for real!! With that kind of start in our relationship, there was nowhere to go but up! She and my father were twenty years old and my big brother, Denim, was barely a year old. By the time our parents turned twenty-four, there would be four of us -- Denim, then me, and our two sisters, Lace and Satin.

My parents had been high school sweethearts and graduated in the same class. Some of our relatives told me that our father and mother were academically at the top of their class. I was proud of them. Their high school success indicated that they probably could have succeeded in college, but the opportunity did not present itself. By nineteen, my parents were married and my brother was on the way. As I got older, I never forgot that sense of pride I felt from their high school accomplishments. It was a part of my motivation to go to college and finish something I believe they both would have loved to accomplish.

But I'm getting ahead of my story, so let me share the joys and wonder I experienced growing up. A portion of my childhood was happy and carefree, at least from a child's perspective. Unlike the world today, the early to late-1950s was a time when kids were safe and free to be kids. I loved summer days spent with Denim, Lace, Satin, my cousin and the other kids on our little dead-end street.

Because it was a dead-end street, we could play ball in the street without worrying about cars. We had trees to climb for anyone interested, lush green wooded areas to explore, shallow sparkling brooks to splash in and catch tadpoles, and we had trails through the woods that led over to our friends' houses on the next street. There were open grassy spaces where, during the day, we could catch June Bugs, tie a long piece of thread on one of their legs and let them fly like a kite through the air. A lot of June Bugs lost their legs that way. At night, those same grassy areas became the perfect place to catch bunches of Fire Flies, put them in a glass jar, put holes in the top with a nail and let them light up like a lantern.

When we went over to the next street to play with friends, my Mother always told us to make sure to come home before the street lights came on or there would be trouble. Occasionally, there was trouble, but grace was usually given. On Sunday, every mother on our street made sure her kids attended Sunday School. We all attended together at the church right on our street.

As kids, my siblings and I were not very aware of the limited earning abilities of our parents. We did not know we were actually classified as "poor." All the families on our street lived, looked and dressed alike, except for one family that had only one child. Their daughter had real toys and nicer clothes. Everyone else had toys made from household items and from nature just like ours. We used paper balls held together by twine, ball bats that were tree limbs and brown paper bags as bases.

Kids then did everything outdoors. One of my favorite things to do with my sisters was to cook a pretend meal. Between the three of us, we always seemed to manage to find a couple of pieces of the one plastic tea set we shared, and to sneak it outside. Often those pieces were never to be seen again, which is why our mother did not want us to take them outside. Sticks from tree branches became our utensils.

There were certain leaves from bushes and trees growing in our yard that we would gather to pretend we were cooking fish or making greens. Mud pies that were dried on a wood board in the hot summer sun became bread, cakes and cookies. Did you know mothers in that day hated mud pies? What a mud pie can do to a kid's clothing was not good! Ask any woman who has made her own mud pies, and she will agree.

Denim was one year and six days older than I. For two years it was just us. Maybe that might explain the special bond I felt with him. As a child, I spent almost all of my playtime with my sisters and he spent almost all of his playtime with a male cousin close to his age. My bond with him was unexplainable, but real. It remains there until this day. When I was fourteen months old and still not walking, my mother said he taught me to walk.

Weighing ten pounds, four ounces at birth may have had some bearing on the situation, but my mother said he was determined to help me walk. She said that after literally hundreds of attempts at physically coaching me to walk, day after day, it happened. He and I were down the hall from where she was when he loudly called out to her that I was walking. I was walking! My mother said when she got down the hallway, I was coming out of the bedroom toddling after my brother. In my mind and heart, he became my hero after hearing that story. It made a huge impact on me and endeared my brother to me in a special way.

I know that I have looked up to him since that day, and followed after him in many ways. I followed him here to Atlanta, where I currently live. He helped me to settle in here thirty-one years ago, and he has been a source of guidance, encouragement and support until this day. Like our Granddaddy, my brother is a man of character, accomplishments, vast knowledge, diverse gifts and abilities, and an abundance of genuine love for his family and all the people in his life. He is a great big brother!

All the kids on our street had two parents. We all had that in common. The little girl who was an only child never had to do the things the rest of us did, such as putting cardboard in our shoes when we needed to fill in the holes on the soles of our shoes. We all had very limited clothing, which meant we wore winter coats that were sometimes too small, and hand-me-downs were considered a blessing. But life was good.

Jobs for my father that provided suitable incomes to support a family were almost non-existent. Jobs for my mother were limited to day work, which included cleaning, cooking and caring for the children of wealthy white women. Taking in laundry and ironing was another option. But at some point, during the first six years of their marriage, my father landed the job as the Director of the Recreation Center for Black people in our town. With a high school diploma, a Certification as a Life Guard, his natural abilities and self-acquired skills in swimming, diving, camping and outdoor life, plus an earned designation as an Eagle Scout, my father was chosen for the job. Our small town was located in the beautiful foothills of western North Carolina and had been the perfect environment for my father to develop and utilize his skills.

Denim, Lace and I were old enough to walk through the woods to the Recreation Center from our home. Satin was still too young. We began filling our summer days with hanging out at the Center, learning to swim, playing on the playgrounds, attending softball games, learning to shoot pool, playing table tennis and other table games. My father allowed me to help run the concession stand and to help sell tickets at the swimming pool. The favorite concession item was two-for-a-penny cookies -- at least they were my favorite.

My love for serving people, social interaction and my awareness of the benefits of recreation and fitness were birthed during those times. The experiences my father allowed us to have at the Center impacted my entire life. Those experiences later influenced me choosing Sociology as my major in college, and eventually led me into a life-long career of serving people.

My favorite happy memory at the Recreation Center was a birthday party my mother planned for Denim, Lace, who was two years younger, and me. Our three birthdays occur during a twenty-four-day span between August and early September. Real birthday parties were unheard of in our family. The only birthday party I ever remember was this one, but it was the birthday party of BIRTHDAY PARTIES!! I was nine, my sister seven and my brother ten.

My Mother's idea was to have one big Swim Party at the Recreation Center. We could each have a cake in our chosen color and we could each invite our classmates from school. The days leading up to that day had to be hard for our mother with the excitement of three children to contend with and our constant chatter and questions about the party. I remember several threats to call the whole thing off if we did not calm down.

The day was getting close, about forty-five kids were invited, and my mother had baked three *Duncan Hines* cakes. Using food color in white frosting, she baked a sunny yellow one for me that was chocolate on the inside, my favorite. She baked a bold blue colored one for my brother Denim and a bright green one for my sister Lace. There would be hot dogs, chips, *Kool-Aid* and, of course, ice cream. I can still vividly remember how excited I was!

When the day came, I was feeling insecure and self-conscious about the way I looked in my navy-blue tank styled swimsuit. My Mother described me as just being a little chubby. She said I would grow out of it. I was not bothered too much about it before, but this big birthday party was happening after *things had changed*. I shifted my thoughts back to the party and all my friends who were coming and how much fun it would be.

My excitement returned. I decided I would just mostly stay in the water and keep my tummy sucked in when I had to walk out around the pool deck. That was my solution--suck it in. It was a solution I would continue to use for a large chunk of my lifetime.

So, everything was in order for the party. The kids came early, of course. Most of them lived within walking distance of the Center. My father let them all in the gate of the pool without paying any admission. Needless to say, a birthday party didn't get much better than this for forty-five Black children in 1957. It was mid-August, and the concrete deck around the pool was much too hot for bare feet, so everyone had on colorful flip-flops. I hated flip-flops because they hurt between my toes. There was loud music, sunny blue skies with a soft breeze, a smoking grill full of hot dogs, picnic tables with bright colored tablecloths and all the potato chips and ice-cold red *Kool-Aid* we wanted. The cakes and ice cream were stashed inside the Recreation Center.

All my favorite friends were there, along with my brother's and my sisters' favorite friends. Even Satin was there looking totally overwhelmed with all the cannon ball jumps into the pool, the splashing, throwing and spitting of water, girls screaming about not getting their hair wet, boys acting like water monsters and wrestling with each other. Good thing there was a baby size pool for the kids Satin's age. It was the best birthday party ever for three of the Williams kids! Ten years later, we were probably still thanking our

8

mother for that party, and our friends talked about it often for years afterwards.

Year round, my maternal grandfather, Waitstill Alexander Tucker, lovingly known as "Granddaddy," made a huge positive impact on my life. Born in 1896, he was a unique and gifted man with a delightful personality. He enlisted in the Army in 1918 and became a Private First Class fighting in World War I. He was a member of one of the first Black units to fight on European soil. He received the Victory Medal of Honor for his service in the Army. Historical information on his life can be found in a small County Museum located in downtown Morganton, NC. There are trees and hedges still standing in our downtown residential and business areas today that he planted many years ago. My siblings and I are so proud when we get a chance to meet up in our hometown and see the legacy he left for everyone.

Granddaddy's love of lawn care, tree planting and gardening was evident around the yard our house shared with his house. He took great pride in the appearance of the yard and was a master at manicuring hedges and trimming trees and shrubs. He was also skilled in carpentry and home repairs. He was known around our town for his skills in these areas. He earned income from providing his services to townspeople, and he became known as a man of quality workmanship, character and integrity.

Because of him, my parents, siblings, an aunt and cousins who lived with him enjoyed eating a variety of fruit from the trees he planted around our yard. There were cherry and fig trees that bore fruit in the summer. In late summer and early fall there were was an apple tree and grape vines loaded with large bunches of sweet grapes and a large pear tree close by that was weighed down with delicious pears every fall. The supply of vegetables from his garden kept my grandmother and my mother canning during the summer in our small houses without any air conditioning.

I loved, admired and respected my Granddaddy a great deal. He had a love for God, family, other people, the church, the land and especially fishing and hunting. Together with his father, Amos Tucker, my grandfather appealed to another African-American man in our town to assist them in building a Presbyterian Church on our street. With this man's help, Green Street Presbyterian Church was completed in 1936. My Great-granddaddy, Amos, served as the church's first superintendent. After his father passed, my Granddaddy became superintendent and an Elder for the church. All the kids on our street attended Sunday School together at Green Street Presbyterian Church. Though very small in size, it is still a functioning Presbyterian church today.

I loved to see Granddaddy smile, which always made me smile. He smiled a lot because he had a wonderful sense of humor and he loved to laugh, especially at himself. I like to think that's where I got my sense of humor. Funny thing is, most of the funny stories he told me were about him. My Granddaddy left our family, community, and me personally with a rich and well-rounded legacy that grows more in value to me as the years pass by.

Chapter 2

School Days

The old saying, "into each life, a little rain must fall" has been very true of my life and everyone else's around me, too. There have been some bitter, rainy days. For the first time, bitter rain began to fall in my young life just prior to the Big Williams Kids' Birthday Party. Without any power to stop it, I saw my life drastically change. I tried to stop the bitter rain in the same way I tried to solve my swimsuit problem at the pool party. I sucked it in, buried it and silently kept going. It would be more than three decades later that *He* would reappear in my life to help me to finally exhale.

Nobody knew that my father had begun sexually molesting me when I was eight years old. It ended at twelve-years-old. It would be a self-destructive secret I kept for forty years. Four years of my young life had been "sucked in" and was deposited in a secret keg, sealed up tightly and buried deep inside me. The emotional cost and damage grew over the years, as I tried to tightly hold the lid on that keg in place.

I hated what was happening to me. It felt like torturous punishment. I began thinking of it as punishment, but I did not know what I had done to be punished like that. He was my father, someone I thought loved me, but I knew that what he was doing wasn't out of love. In my little girl mind, I tried to figure out why my father didn't love me anymore, and I tried to figure out what I could do to get him to love me again and stop what he was doing to me.

At home, I was secretly striving to become the perfect daughter, always working hard to be helpful. I was always looking for ways to try to stop the torturous punishment. Being the oldest girl was a position I thought I could use to show my father what a good girl I was. "Look at me," I thought. "Look at how well behaved, hardworking and helpful I am! Don't you see? Look, I am being a good girl!"

In school, I worked hard to get the best grades I could, striving for all A's. My grades were always good. Nothing worked to change my father's abuse. Although, I did receive lots of positive feedback and attention from my mother for my efforts, I never got the results I was desperately hoping for with my father. I kept trying anyway. I thought it was my only way out. The abuse continued.

Then, I remembered what I had learned in Sunday School! I learned that Jesus loved me and was watching over me. I loved that song, *"Jesus Loves Me."* I decided what I could do, and for the briefest moment, I believed I had solved my problem. I asked Jesus to help me! I did. I asked and I asked and I asked. But Jesus didn't stop my father from sexually abusing me.

I don't even remember the day I simply stopped asking. The bitter rain continued to fall, as I thought my heart would literally break. I was too young to realize that God gives us trials to bring out strength inside us that we will need at a later point in our lives. So, I now thought neither God, nor my father loved me. What could I possibly have done to deserve for Him to forsake me? I was utterly confused, and yet every day, I awoke and went through the hours never knowing if that day would bring more of the abuse that was devasting every part of me.

To my absolute astonishment, I soon realized that, even while carrying this kind of pain inside, there was still one place I could always find sweet rain. That place was with my mother, and my siblings, brother Denim and sisters Lace and Satin. I felt loved by them and that love never went away.

I had convinced myself that it had to be something I was doing to deserve the way I was being treated by my father. Somehow, I was convinced it was my fault. I told myself that I could not dare tell my mother. She and my siblings were all I had. I knew that I had her love and I could not risk losing it. That meant I would never reveal my secret to my mother or my siblings, which I thought would guarantee their collective love for me. Therefore, I made up my mind that in the company of Mom, Denim, Lace and Satin, I would always have refuge. That was the sweet rain, and I delighted in every moment when it fell gently upon me and quenched my thirst to be loved.

My reality was that my father no longer loved me, and that Jesus no longer loved me. But the mother and three siblings in my life loved me greatly, and that was enough for me. I didn't know then that God had future plans of His own for me, and for my father, and for the abuse.

During that four-year period from the time I was eight to twelve, I perfected my skill for telling time so that I could figure out when my father would be coming home. Once he came home, I would stay out-side as long as possible and try not to draw his attention when I came inside the house. But once he realized I wasn't telling my mother or anyone else about what he was doing to me, he got bolder.

I endured the bitter rain until that horrible season in my life came to an end four years later. Looking back, I'm aware that just when the sexual abuse stopped in my life, I was entering the age of puberty, where girls and boys get silly thinking about each other and wonder what their first kiss or caress would feel like. My innocence had been taken away!

I didn't see it at the time, of course, but my numerous attempts to win back my father's love so that he would stop abusing me created a pattern of "people pleasing." The people pleasing solution didn't work with my father, but it appeared to be working with my peers. My inability to stand up for myself, being afraid to speak up or give my opinion became routine.

Kids at school and in the neighborhood found me easy to get along with because I never objected to anything they wanted to do. I never offered opposing opinions to anything the group thought or did.

Nobody could find fault with me, so I was accepted as the quiet member of every group to which I sought to belong. I was almost invisible, but at least I was "in." People pleasing would later become my means of getting to belong in "people circles," where I did not feel I was worthy to belong on my own merits for years to come.

Navigating school academically was never a big problem for me. But my elementary school years had its share of bitter rain drizzle to add to my already immense supply of insecurities. My bitter rain days in elementary school had to do with how I looked. I describe my skin color as the color of chocolate, just like my mother's. So, both my mother and I fell short of being identified as beautiful because we could not pass the "color" standard. There was an unspoken, but obvious skin color bias that existed in the African American community. It still exists today and is still kept quiet. I first experienced it in my first-grade class and it would be felt many more times in my life. It caused further hurt and damage to my already deflated self-image.

A girl in my first-grade class who became my best first grade friend had a very light complexion and beautiful wavy hair. When the teacher would ask for help, both our hands would fly up, as well as other kids' hands in the class. But my best friend or another light-skinned classmate was the one most often chosen. I wanted to help too, but the children with the lighter skin were more often chosen as classroom helpers and leaders during class activities.

They were also more likely to have leading parts in school plays and other school performances. A saying in our African-American Community after I became a teen-ager was, *"If you are white, you're right....If you are black, get back....If you are brown stick around."* The standard of the color bias was that children whose complexions were the color of a brown paper bag or lighter were favored above children whose skin color was darker than a brown paper bag.

Denim, Lace and Satin took their complexion color after our father. They would pass the brown paper bag test. My mother and I failed, but fortunately, the bitter rain of the skin color bias never fell on me at home. We were all treated the same at home. But that difference was present when we would visit with some of my father's extended family.

The reception and amount of attention my siblings got was greater, warmer and much more inviting than what I received. No one else ever seemed to notice, but for me, it was something else I had to suck in, just as I sucked in my stomach at my pool birthday party, and just as I had to suck in my desire to scream out loud when my father abused me for four years. I had to keep smiling, even when I felt hurt. I wanted my relatives to like me too, but since that was never going to happen for me, I endured what became deepening wounds in silence. On those visits, I would stick close to my mother. I was so thankful that she was the color of chocolate too.

By age twelve, the pressure in the keg that held my deepest and saddest emotions had started to build. Thoughts of what the four years of sexual abuse felt like began recurring in my mind and terrorizing me. In my head, I pictured my future as a messed-up nightmare one moment, and a blank void the next. Keeping it sucked in was taking more and more effort, and it was draining me emotionally.

Still holding the lid down on the keg, I was about to enter my teenage season lacking everything a teenage girl needed to survive, except a mother's love. I knew my mother loved me. That was my sweet rain. Somehow sucking it in had been simpler as a young child. It became more complicated and more difficult as I got older.

But, my secret keg was not the only object of secrecy and pain present in our family. By this time, there was pressure caused by problems in my parents' marriage. I could hear and feel the pressure building between them. My father's drinking habit had escalated and created a pressure pot. When at home with us, my father seemed discontent, impatient, critical and grumpy, but with the children and adults at the Recreation Center or in our neighborhood, he smiled and was pleasant and talkative.

This had to feel like bitter rain to my mother. I knew she wanted him to relate to us in the same way, but it never happened. My brother and I saw the difference in how he treated us compared to how he treated our friends or even children he did not know. My brother and I could both feel the bitter rain falling at those times, but we never spoke about it as children. Later in life, we would, but in those days, we both sucked it in.

Arguments between my parents escalated. My mother tried to keep the peace. Finally, the marriage "keg" blew! It was a night of bitter rain that I would never, ever forget. It was a warm night. We were all at home. The four of us were in the bedroom we shared. I could overhear them talking and could tell they were arguing. The usual dread, stress and anxiety set in when I heard them arguing. I listened, hoping it would stop. It didn't stop. Instead it escalated as they moved out onto our front porch.

I could hear and see from the open widow of the bedroom. My father had told my mother he was moving away. My mother was crying and begging my father to stay. He started down the steps of the front porch and began to walk out the driveway, with my mother walking alongside him, pleading with him to stay. When he kept walking, my mother tried to stop him by holding onto him. As she grabbed hold of him, he continued to walk. She stumbled and grabbed hold of one of his legs and would not let go. She wrapped her arms around his leg as he continued to walk away. He was dragging her out of the driveway as she cried, *"Please don't go, please don't leave."*

My father did not stop. He kept walking. My mother finally let go of his leg. She got to her feet and I ran out to meet her. We walked back toward the house. There were no words spoken, but my mind and heart were racing. I do not remember if Denim, Lace and Satin were out there or what was happening with them. The memory of the sights and sounds of my mother coming apart like that would remain in my heart forever. A torrent of bitter rain fell that night for my mother and for me. My heart hurt for my mother. It was the most emotionally agonizing experience I could imagine witnessing my mother ever going through.

My heart broke for her, but in the same moment, I was lost in my own personal whirlpool of uncontrollable emotions. While my mother was in agony over my father's departure, I was thinking, "I am glad he is leaving." I thought, "Finally the nightmare of my life could be over." Yes, I felt relieved he was leaving and I hoped he would never return. But, with that feeling of relief came a tormenting backlash of guilt for being happy while my mother was so sad. I was twelve. I could not handle that overwhelming feeling of guilt. So, I sucked in the guilt, and slammed the lid on the keg shut forever! Wham!!

Gone was my broken heart, torment, shame, rejection, fears, feelings of loss and guilt, or so I thought. With the lid slammed tightly on the keg, I unconsciously began a campaign to make it all go away forever. Only one tool was used to clamp that lid down tight and relieve me from the burden of holding it shut. That tool was "denial." It took time to get the desired results, but with my desperation to just forget all of it, my new tool began to work. It would work well for years, but not forever.

Somewhere along the way, I had become totally convinced that what happened to me was my fault. I did not understand the depth of my mother's love for me. I never told my mother what was happening to me, in spite of knowing with absolute certainty that she loved me. I was too afraid of losing her love. I felt an incredible amount of shame from being abused. Now, I felt guilty for being glad when my father left. I was bound by a triple locked grip of fear, shame and guilt.

If I ever had any positive feelings or thoughts about myself, they melted away like new snow in the warm sunshine. At this point, my descent into denial was equivalent to cutting off my oxygen and suffocating myself emotionally. But, denial became my only hope of survival. What I didn't know was that the denial I was descending into had an expiration date. The expiration date would coincide with His arrival back into my life.

I convinced myself that I was prepared for any future emotional issues that should come along. My tools for navigating my life had become to continue to sharpen my people pleasing skills and to build on and fine-tune my denial skills. In other words, never "go there" again. How people made me feel became my chief indicator of my value and worth. Moving forward from that point, my main objective unconsciously became to make sure people liked me all the time.

Without knowing it, I entered my teenage season lacking everything a teenage girl needs to survive, except her mother's love. I knew my mother loved me. My father had moved out of state and I had found my new best friend -- "denial." It seemed like a new start.

My denial solution quenched my desire to bury the pain of my past, but denial could not stop the pain headed my way in my future. I had no idea that being rejected by my father would become the most damaging component of his abuse. I had never experienced love or validity from my father, only feelings of pain from his rejection. It tore open a hole in my heart and birthed an unstoppable and unconscious desire to be loved and validated by a man. Unfortunately, this uncontrollable desire inside me would position me for more devastating hurt from the men whom I allowed to enter my life until I learned how to protect myself. With every rejection from a man came more devastating feelings of rejection, hurt and loss of self-value. But, years later, I would learn how to survive and how to protect myself from men.

The distractions of high school were a welcomed relief. I utilized the only strengths I thought I had. Basically, my social skills, basketball skills, ability to carry a tune and my okay academic ability were my strengths. These things got me through my high school years. In reality those days could only be called bittersweet rain days because my unhealthy people pleasing robbed me of having healthy, balanced relationships. Also, my basketball ability was hindered by my lack of self-confidence. I did well in the high school choir and okay with my grades.

Late in my junior year, with everything all deposited safely into the keg deeply nestled in a corner of my mind, I met the first and only man I would ever really love. His name was Suede. He was also a junior, but our romance blossomed during our senior year, the year Black students were integrated into formerly all-white schools for the first time.

Suede played football and basketball, had decent grades, sang in the choir, was college bound, and was very popular with the guys and the girls, of course. His skin color was deep chocolate. He stood about six feet tall, was well built, had a wonderful smile, and dark, dreamy eyes with long eyelashes that were almost hidden behind his glasses. We knew each other. We lived only a short distance from each other, and we had some of the same interests in high school.

Even though there was plenty of competition for his attention, somehow we hit it off and began to talk some early mornings at school before our classes began. At the new school where the Black kids were bussed, there was an open breezeway on the second floor of our brick school building that looked out on the front street below.

Most students entered the building from the front. There was always at least a gentle breeze coming through the breezeway. It was cool during the warm months and cold during the fall and winter months. No matter what the weather, I would wait and watch for him to arrive, but not in view where he could see me. My hope everyday was that he would enter and take the stair up to that breezeway to get to where he was going. Some days, he would come that way and stop to talk with me for a while.

Those were sweet rain days for me, for sure. I fell in love for my first and only time, at least so far. Things grew gradually from there and we ended up in a relationship that spanned forty-five years of our lives. Our overall relationship would be more accurately described as bitter sweet.

As in most relationships, there was a mixture of both sweet rain and bitter rain. Our bitter and sweet relationship included us remaining sweethearts throughout our college days, returning to our home town where we started our work careers, and eventually getting married and having our daughter who became the delight of both our lives. I will tell you more about our adult lives together later in our road trip.

The bitter rain began to fall our senior year of high school. We were spending time together at school before classes and a little after school. We had both made the varsity basketball teams. I saw us as boyfriend and girlfriend, even though it was never directly discussed. A new dynamic was added to his popularity with girls at this new, integrated school. A particular white girl in our senior class began pursuing him, and her best friend began pursuing his best friend who also played basketball. Since these girls were openly and aggressively making their interest in them known, the gossip got back to me quickly.

I immediately began to feel threatened and insecure by this gossip, and I asked him if he was interested in the girl. Of course, his answer was, "No," but I already had started feeling very upset and suspicious about his relationship with her. She was pretty and I immediately began comparing myself to her. The thoughts that she was white and that attention from her would top any attention I was giving him became my reality.

The brown bag test quickly came back to my mind and I knew I would fail the brown bag test in this competition for sure. And that was only the skin competition. I didn't dare focus on the hair competition, nor the natural boldness that all white students seemed to possess. I was out of my league, just like that!

With my lack of self-confidence and my low level of self-value, it did not take long for me to convince myself that he was not being truthful with me. I began thinking about and feeling the hurt of being rejected by him, although we were still seeing each other. In the background, the rumors were that these girls had been spotted cruising through his neighborhood. Suede and his friend lived a very short distance from each other. I lived just over the hill from them both.

The gossipers were saying that these girl's drives through our neighborhood had become more frequent and had turned into "stop and talk" meetings on the corner next to Suede's house. The rumors became reality when I saw the two girls parked on the corner right next to his house. I was devastated and heart- broken when I saw them there. There was no longer any doubt in my mind -- she was in and I was out.

The story from him was that they were there waiting on his best friend to come over to meet her friend. He said he was not involved with her. The damage was still done. My trust in him was destroyed that day. All I could feel was the pain of rejection.

For the first time since feeling the pain of rejection from my father, that special kind of pain was back. For me, it was real and it was devastating. But, in spite of the pain of the rejection I was feeling, I remained in the relationship with him after hearing him say he did not want to break up with me. I settled for that and continued the relationship, thinking that our senior year would be ending soon and we would be leaving for college.

Sucking it in came back again as the only and correct solution to accepting the failure of my first relationship with a male. I sucked in my hurt and disappointment, locked it down and kept it moving, thinking that college would solve this problem. I will pick back up from here later on in the road trip, because there is so much more to tell about my senior year in high school.

Chapter 3

The Racism Blues

There was a monumental change at my high school and every other school in the State of North Carolina in the year 1965-66. It was the year of the integration of schools. There were several all-white elementary, middle and high schools spread throughout our county, but all the Black kids who lived throughout the city and out in the country attended the same all-Black elementary, middle and high schools designated for us. These schools were located inside the city of Morganton.

Integration separated us, after spending our entire school careers together to that point. We were sent to schools formerly attended by only white students. My brother, Denim, would not be affected by the integration because he would graduate in the current school year, 1965. His class was the last class to graduate from our beloved

Olive Hill High School. However, Lace and Satin and I were integrated into new schools.

I could not believe I would be spending my highly celebrated senior year of high school in a foreign, hostile, racially charged and maybe even unsafe environment, and neither could my approximately two-hundred Black rising senior classmates. I lived inside the city and was assigned to attend the largest and most popular high school in Burke County. The Black seniors who lived out of the city in the country areas would be transferred to the high schools closest to them.

Our beloved *Olive Hill High School* would be emptied out and closed down. All of us who were being transferred would be the first Black kids who would ever walk in the hallways, eat in the cafeteria, cram stuff in the lockers, sit in the classrooms and look into the faces of those white teachers at those newly integrated schools. The most unbelievable and disappointing thing for us was that it was happening our senior year. It was too much for me to wrap my mind around. All of that sounded like bitter rain to me.

Over the summer leading up to the integration, the city newspaper tried to play it up as a harmonious new beginning. I was not feeling harmonious, I was feeling ripped off. There would be no keeping of our senior year traditions. There would be no senior prom or graduation filled with our own traditions, customs or the style we were accustomed to. It was a change that none of the students wanted to see happen. Not us and not them! That bitter rain had turned into a tidal wave of change headed right at me, and there was nothing I could do but try to ride the tide and hope to make it to the shore.

But some sweet rain came when my mind cleared enough to realize, I would not be alone. I believe there were about fifty of us who transferred. We were mandated by law to attend that school but it felt more like being high jacked against our will.

Over that summer, I had to make two big personal decisions regarding my last year of high school and my transfer to this new school. With my mother's support and encouragement, decision number one was made. I decided that I wanted to press forward with my dream of attending college, in spite of how my senior year went at this school. My grades had been good up until that point, but I knew the school change would probably bring some difficult and maybe unfair academic challenges. When the challenges arrived, they exceeded my expectation, and not in a good way.

There had been some tense times throughout our county for Blacks. We had experienced our share of racism and discrimination. I can't remember exactly what age I was when my mother first took me to *Woolworth's*, a popular store that would resemble a *Walmart* today, but much smaller. Unlike *Walmart*, *Woolworth's* had a lunch counter where people could purchase food and sit and eat. That day my mother treated me to my first *Woolworth's* hot dog. Spending money on a hot dog in a store was a very rare and special treat. I think I remember them costing about twenty cents each. The hot dog vendor was on one of the aisles in the store. It never occurred to me that it was a strange location for selling hot dogs.

After we got our hot dogs, we were standing in the aisle eating them. I saw people sitting at the lunch counter and suggested we go sit down and eat our hot dogs. After my mother explained why we could not do that, I was a little confused. I was looking at people eating at the snack bar and we were people. It did not make sense to me that some people could eat there and other people could not, just because of their skin color, but then I remembered the brown paper bag test. Years later, I participated in a sit-in and boycott at that *Woolworth's* lunch bar that eventually led to a new day. The day came when my mother and I went back there, bought our hot dogs and sat at that lunch counter. I think we had a Coke too!

Experiencing racism firsthand with my mother at that *Woolworth's* store reminded me of other tender, hurtful moments where I knew for certain that I was the victim of discrimination, and worse, that I was powerless to do anything about it. Once while in middle school, four or five of us were walking home from an evening school event. We were walking through the downtown area when a car came by and the white people inside it threw raw eggs at us and called us the N-word. We were shocked and frightened. We turned the first corner we came to and tried to stay out of sight until we got back into our neighborhood.

Ku Klux Klan activity was not an uncommon occurrence around our county during my childhood and later on. Only about 10% of the Burke County population at that time was Black. There were a few communities and areas around the county that were known for racist activities and hatred of Blacks. There was one particular community that made its hatred of Blacks known publicly. So all the Blacks I knew stayed clear of that area, sometimes walking or riding a good distance out of our way to get to a destination. Life was just that dangerous if you were Black.

The second decision I had to make regarding my senior year as one of the first Blacks to be integrated into an all-white high school related to racism. The question was whether or not I would try out for the girls' basketball team at the integrated school. My mother had played basketball in high school. From what I was told, she was a star basketball player on her team. She had skills, was self-confident, and was not afraid to be aggressive. I never had her level of skill, self-confidence or aggressiveness, but I decided I wanted to try out for the team and just see what happened. My strengths were my height, my implementation of defensive strategies and my good reflexes for blocking shots.

As the days ticked by over the summer, anxiety over the integration increased. The talk around town indicated that parents on both sides were on edge. As the opening day got closer, I could feel the tension in the air like a tight rubber band stretched to the max. It was the topic of conversation for almost everyone. I did not have a good feeling about the integration at all, and neither did anyone else I knew. My mother was also a little anxious and concerned about our safety. The first day came. A couple of other friends and I walked there together, thinking there is safety in numbers.

The school was a two-story brick building. It was the largest high school in the county. It was four to five times larger than our beloved school. It was located in downtown Morganton, across the street from the hospital and a few minutes walk from City Hall and the Police Department. Our main downtown area was also within walking distance.

Approximately, fifty Black seniors were assigned to this school, along with two Black teachers. One Black teacher taught Biology and the other taught Math. There were about three hundred white seniors in the class. Once the first day enrollment process began that day, our little fifty got scattered like sheep. Things were moving so fast that we did not have time to even look for each other. That was day one and it never slowed down, not during the entire school year.

I do not recall attending any kind of pre-orientation class. Everything about the school was new to me. Getting enrolled and finding my classes was very stressful and frustrating without any help. No help was provided, only written instructions. One or two of the white students I encountered tried to be helpful, but the majority of them were acting like I was invisible.

There was a significant chill in the air and it had nothing to do with the air conditioning. It was a cold and hostile environment, and that was not my mind playing tricks on me. I know it was not my mind playing tricks because when I ran into any of the other forty-nine who came with me, they were reporting the same problems. No one would even make eye contact with me, no less, let me get close enough to employ my now-perfected people pleasing skills. If I had become able to please anybody in that school, I could have won the Nobel Peace Prize.

When my classes began, I quickly recognized, that from the teachers' perspective, it was going to be a long year. Only one of my teachers even acknowledged my presence in class. It was going to be a "sink or swim" year for sure. Our group of fifty could hardly be found on the radar screen. It became a full-blown celebration when two of us landed in a class together or ran into each other in the hallways. I could see and feel the resentment in people's eyes.

Denial had already become my best friend and was the primary reason I survived that environment for a year. For me, every school day there included a few sprinkles of bitter rain, but my school days ended with going home where my mother and siblings always had a little sweet rain waiting. And I still had that relationship with my dark chocolate fellow senior, with whom I had bonded since our junior year together.

I made the girls' basketball team and so did another Black girl who was a friend of mine. We were the only Black girls on the team. Playing on the basketball team and going to practice turned out to be the only enjoyable activity I would experience at that school. Our coach was a female teacher who was knowledgeable in basketball and in coaching. It appeared to me that she wanted to build a good team.

From the beginning, her treatment of the girls on the team was impartial and without favoritism, which I wasn't expecting to see. But because of her character, personality and leadership style, I felt at ease being on the team. My friend and I were pleased that we were actually becoming a real part of the team. The team was coming together and working hard. The goal the coach had set for us was to become the Division Champions for 1966. Based on their prior record and the combined skills on our team, we had a shot at winning the championship.

There were about fourteen girls on the team altogether. The starting team was chosen. I made the starting team, along with four white seniors and a junior. The four senior girls were hyped up to win the championship because it was their last year and they wanted to finish strong. Our coach reported that we had several tough teams to defeat on the road to that championship. As a team, we agreed to make winning that championship our goal.

The game schedule was published with the names of our opposing schools and the dates for the games. Practice sessions leading up to each game were comprised of our coach identifying the strengths and weaknesses of our team, compared to the strengths and weaknesses of our opposing team. She gave us a strategy for maximizing our strengths and for strengthening our weaknesses. Our job at each practice was to focus on honing the individual and collective skills we would need to win the next game. When our individual and team skills synergized well, we performed well and we usually won the game.

Prior to the season beginning, our coach instructed my friend and I on what to expect when we stepped off the bus or entered the gyms of our opposing team. She instructed us on safety measures we would have to take because we were Black. Rule One was not to ever go into the locker rooms after the games. We were to stay in our bench area at all times. Rule Two was to be prepared for verbal harassment and jeering from the fans.

Along with those instructions came our coach's physically watching over us. She kept close eyes on us, making sure of our whereabouts at all times during the games. Her instructions informed and warned us, but could not incubate us from the feelings resulting from being harassed and jeered by hate-filled fans. There were schools in our school district that we would play that had no Black players. Many of the fans at these schools were vehemently opposed to seeing Blacks physically compete with their white players, and they often vocalized their objections in the meanest way possible during the games.

Tensions ran very high at games played at high schools in communities in our county and in districts that were racist. Our team weathered these experiences, and as a team we went on to win that Divisional Championship. The four senior girls on the team were elated and very proud to be a part of providing their school with this significant good-bye gift. I was glad I had become part of the team, and I was proud that I went all the way. I finished my high school basketball career on the basketball court my senior year like I had done the three preceding years. It was a little sweet rain I brought myself during a year when I really, really needed it.

I have spoken with our old basketball coach by phone two or three times in recent years, and we exchanged a couple of emails. Her name is Mrs. Maxine Amos. When we last talked, she was still healthy and well. She had reached out to me to tell me about a wonderful visit she had from some of my former teammates.

There had been a high school reunion for the school, and sometime during the reunion weekend, the four senior girls from our starting team had driven over to her city from our hometown to see her. She was delighted to see them and so excited to tell me about it.

I could hear the joy in her voice as she described her visit with them. She asked why I did not come, and was saying how great it would have been to see me, along with my friend who also made the team.

Perhaps I was uncomfortable explaining to the coach I had come to admire that I felt certain I would not have been received with the same enthusiasm as the four white girls from the team were received. Perhaps I didn't think she would understand the level of racism that could persist into adulthood for most of the people connected to that integrated high school.

Regardless, I told her she made a positive impact on me in a place and time where acceptance and caring were almost non-existent. I told her that her unprejudiced response to me shined brightly in that place and time, and it would always be remembered. I found sweet rain in an amazingly difficult senior year through my basketball coach.

But, I also needed to be truthful in answering her initial question. I had to examine my heart to determine exactly why I didn't come to the high school reunion. I decided she would understand if I answered her question by sharing my reality. From her perspective, I am sure she assumed that I had bonded in friendship with the girls that visited with her and others on the team. She saw us as teammates. Surely her winning team had accomplished a wonderful goal and, in the process, we had naturally become friends. We had not.

I honestly and gently tried to explain my view of the team. The only goal we shared was becoming a winning team. There was never a goal to become friends on any of our parts. I feel sure we all unconsciously knew bonding in friendship under those circumstances during that year was not realistic. The complicated social dynamics, background differences and time limitations were close to impossible to overcome.

But, I am also sure that if I ever encounter any one of them again, I would consider them a friend and treat them as such. I would tell them that I am thankful for the experience of being a part of that team. It is a sweet rain memory for me, especially when I show my pictures from the newspaper and share my story with my young grandchildren today.

Winning the basketball championship was memorable, but there was a grander event that got much more attention. It was our graduation ceremony, which may have been a sweet rain memory for some, but it was a stress-filled degrading nightmare for others. Nothing could have been more callous and mean-spirited than what was done at our graduation ceremony.

We had heard the rumor that supposedly graduating seniors could be eliminated from graduating, even while standing in line, dressed in cap and gown and ready to proceed out on the field where family and friends were waiting in the stands. I did not believe that could happen. I dismissed it as vicious gossip aimed at ruining what should be one of the most significant days in our lives. I thought, "No way that is going to happen!" But, it did.

Too much had already happened to us. First, a portion of our Black seniors never even came to this school. Some of them opted out and went to earn their GED from the community college in town. Others gave up and settled for an 11th grade education. Second, another portion gave up after arriving, and they dropped out due to the difficulty encountered in trying to pass the courses.

I believe the bar for passing the courses was raised in honor of our arrival. In addition, it appeared as if the teaching staff had taken an oath to be as little help as possible to us. I had flunked French and had barely passed math without anyone noticing except me. It really was a "sink or swim" situation.

Just now, as I write this part of my story, I realize that God made a way for me through my ordeals, so that given this hostile, racist environment in which I found myself, I was able to survive academically, and to thrive athletically. He did that because He knew I was His Girl, and He also knew that in time, I would come to see myself the way He saw me.

As we stood in that line, just outside the fence to the field, I could hear a commotion behind me. It was really happening. There were staff members from the school walking up the line, stopping and informing some seniors that they could not graduate. They had to drop out of the line immediately, leaving their family members waiting in the stands to see them graduate. We were lined up in alphabetical order. I froze, my heart froze, and my mind was spinning out of control.

All I could think was, "Please no, please no, please no," knowing something else could have gone down with another one of my grades and if it did, I would be out of there. No human teenager should have to feel what I felt. It was mental and emotional torture during those agonizing minutes.

They were getting closer to me. When I looked down, with my peripheral vision keener than ever, I could see their feet moving in my direction. They passed by me. My knees felt like they were going to buckle, my heart was racing, I wanted to cry, and tears started running down my face. I felt exhausted and just wanted to get this whole mess over with and go home.

I never looked back to see whose shoulders got tapped. Looking back to see would have added more cruelty to the horrible thing that was already happening to some of the seniors in that line. I was heartbroken for those who had to leave the line, and I was sorry for their family members who would be so disappointed. Rumors were that actually some white and Black seniors were pulled from the line, but I did not want to know or ask or hear their names. Perpetuating or adding to the humiliation of any of them by seeking to find out who they were was unthinkable to me.

In retrospect, I know they were pulled because they hadn't met all the requirements for graduation. Isn't it up to those qualified, highly educated guidance counselors, teachers and administrators to have found out that information and conveyed it to the affected students and their parents *before* graduation day? Racism aside, that's plain incompetent and those adults should have been held accountable for the cruelty they exhibited towards their students.

The whole graduation thing and most of that year got sucked inside that secret keg I had hidden away deep inside me. It landed in my "forget it file" inside my denial keg. The whole ordeal felt like a bitter hurricane with lingering downpours throughout the ceremony. I felt no joy, not even when I held my diploma in my hand. At that moment, I felt exhausted and sad. At least it was over, I thought. I just wanted to go home. I knew I could always find a little sweet rain there, and I did.

Over the years since then, I have often wondered how many Black seniors arrived at that school, and how many of us actually graduated. The numbers have never been published to my knowledge, but based on our graduation picture that was taken before graduation night, I would say about twenty, which would be less than half. And let's not forget those who decided against even attending that integrated school, and those who entered and left shortly afterwards.

There are no statistics because nobody cared about the number of Blacks who might have earned their high school diplomas if they had stayed in their segregated high schools and communities. The not-so-subtle objective was always to deny as many Blacks as possible the opportunity to become successful adults, beginning with the acquisition of high school diplomas. Systemic racism is designed to steal, kill and destroy dreams, hopes and futures for persons of color. But God was and still is so much bigger than racism and He always has a plan!!!

Looking back on it, years later, I realize that we did have one thing in common with some of the white seniors. Like us, some of them were overwhelmed, angry and resentful because of the flood of changes in their school lives that were beyond their control. We had that in common, but we lacked the wisdom at that time to understand it, and we certainly lacked the opportunity or the time to realize it.

Because of having more time together, the junior, sophomore and freshmen classes behind us had more opportunities to turn some of their bitter rain into sweet rain. The good news is that things did get better. I know that relationships among the students were better when Lace graduated from the school two years later, and it had continued to improve when Satin graduated from the school four years later.

Sweet rain fell again for me later when, after working for a year after high school, I was finally able to go off to college, as I had always dreamed of doing. College was where I began my "great escape." I believed I had left the past behind, that I had survived it all and was getting a new start. But I should have remembered, or at least taken into account that my best friend, "denial" was very deceptive.

Chapter 4

Fake News

After Jesus's re-entry into my life as an adult, I realized I had been insecure and lacking self-confidence before my father began abusing me. I could not recall anything that happened prior to the abuse to make me feel so devalued. Maybe it was innate. But from the beginning of the abuse and my decision to suck it in, the lid on that invisible keg in my young mind became compromised by the life that would still happen around me over the years.

I did not feel the keg pressure as greatly in my childhood, maybe because a child's mind has a protective device for handling emotional pain and trauma. That would explain why with the passing of each season of my life, it became more difficult for me to hold down the lid on the keg.

It had been five years since my father left. We all survived his departure. The only thing missing at this point in my life was

Denim. He had graduated high school the year before me. His class was the last class to graduate from our beloved high school, so he did not have to endure all the fear, rejection, and real trauma of those of us who were sent to the "right" school where we were viewed daily as "wrong."

Denim enlisted in the Navy soon after graduating. He was in San Diego, California for basic training and was very excited about the possibility of seeing different parts of the world. It was the first time he had been away from home. He sent us post cards describing his new adventures in the Navy. My favorite days at home were the days we got mail from him. Those were sweet rain days.

I missed Denim a lot and talked about him every day, especially at meal times. His spot at the table was empty, but the cabinets and refrigerator were fuller than they had ever been before. As kids, my sisters and I called Denim the "bottomless pit" because he could eat so much. We could not believe how much he could eat. Even at nine years old and skinny as a coat hanger, Denim insured that a box of *Cheerios* and a quart of milk never had a chance with him. He could eat a whole honey bun in one bite.

He was a wonderful big brother whom we missed every day, and whom we so greatly loved. After his three years in the Navy, his adventurous lifestyle continued, but holidays always brought him home to us. These were always happy times for the family. I found a satisfying joy in seeing us all together.

My mother loved the holidays and always managed to make them special sweet rain days, even with the meager income she was able to bring in at that point. All her attempts to persuade my father to send us reliable on-going financial help failed, so what she earned was all we could ever really count on. My fathers' every now and then funds were sporadic. Mom stretched every dollar she could earn to the max. We ate a lot of oatmeal, grits, whole cake bread, potatoes and soup made with neckbones. If you have never eaten neckbones, there is a good reason they are called neck bones!

As time marched on, some better job opportunities began to open up for Blacks in our town. My mother immediately applied for a job when *Carolina Shoe Company* began hiring women to do production work. That opportunity came as a result of the huge demand for combat boots for the soldiers fighting in the Vietnam War. Some of the boys who graduated in my senior class had been drafted, including Suede's long-time best friend. The Vietnam War would become the source of a long season of bitter rain for some of the soldiers who fought there, as well as for their families. We were so relieved that Denim had already enlisted in the Navy. He was never deployed to Vietnam.

It is said that men make money during a war. *Carolina Shoe Company* made a bundle of it. My mother got hired, and for several months she made more money than she had ever made before. She was working on the combat boot assembly line where you were paid according to what you could produce. The more you produced the more money you made. My mother was strong and fit. She set a production goal for herself, and her hard work paid off each week until she began having pain in her hands. Eventually the demand of constantly using her hands in such a repetitive manner became too painful to endure. She had to give up the job.

But not long after that, another new job opportunity for Blacks had been announced at a local hospital. *Broughton Hospital*, a specialized hospital for adults with mental health disorders, announced they were hiring Dietary Aides. *Broughton Hospital* was a large, state-owned residential facility for the mentally ill that served hundreds of patients from around the entire state of North Carolina. It was a major opportunity for Blacks, one that opened up as a result of the E*conomic Opportunity Act of 1964.*

For the first time in our city, Blacks would have an equal opportunity for being hired for these state jobs, and my mother was one of the first to apply and to get hired. The Dietary Aide position and salary was at the bottom of the totem pole, along with their housekeeping jobs, but it included medical insurance, paid vacations and paid sick leave. A whole new world of employment opportunities, benefits and possibilities had opened up for all the Blacks in our county, as well as the entire nation.

After several years in the Dietary Department, my mother heard of a new position that she would qualify to apply for within

Broughton Hospital. It was a Health Care Technician, which focused on the direct daily care of the patients on the hospital wards. With an excellent recommendation from her Dietary Department supervisor, my mother applied and was offered a Health Care Technician position, which she gratefully accepted. Many years later, my mother became one of the first two Blacks to achieve a supervisory position at *Broughton Hospital.* She became a supervisor for both the White and Black Health Care Technicians. Our whole family was bursting with pride, due to her achievements and her advancement with high recommendations from her previous supervisors. After thirty-years of service, my mother retired from *Broughton Hospital.*

As I said earlier, my mother carried the financial burden for providing for us. When my brother, Denim joined the Navy, Lace, Satin and I were, of course, still at home. A few months into my senior year of high school, it became obvious that there was no chance of my mother having money for me to go to college. But my dream to go remained intact, despite the fact that I had no idea how I would get the money for college.

My mother came up with a proposal. Her plan required a commitment from us both. Her proposal was that if I would work for the next year and saved all that I could for college, then she would save all she could after the bills and family expenses were paid, and she would put any extra money into a college fund that we would combine at the end of the year for my college expenses.

I went ahead and notified *North Carolina College* in Durham, N.C. that I needed to delay my entry until the next year. Our hope was that we could save at least enough to cover my first semester at NCC, where I had already been accepted. I not only liked my mothers' idea, but also, I was very grateful for the hope it provided. My dream still had a chance.

Her proposal led me to immediately start looking for a job as soon as I could after graduating high school. I did not have to look long. With business booming at *Carolina Shoe Company*, I applied for and landed a job with them as a Conveyer Belt Operator. The factory was huge, but all of the work stations were under one roof. As soon as you opened the door to go in, the smell of boot leather filled your nose, and the noise filled your ears. At the end of the day, I smelled like boot leather, my hands and cloths were grimy and I could not wait to be in a quiet place. Because of hundreds of machines working simultaneously, the noise level was constantly so loud that people had to get in very close to hear each other.

The job paid above minimum wage, which was very good for a seventeen-year old girl, but it was not a lightweight job. It was an adult-sized job. The job required a great deal of physical strength and endurance, the ability to handle stress, good memorization ability, social skills, organizational skills, the ability to multi-task and pay attention to details, self-discipline and a tolerance for constant noise.

It was a physically demanding job that often required overtime because of the high demand for the combat boots we produced. As a Conveyor Belt Operator, I had the responsibility for sending large, heavy plastic cartons of combat boot parts to about twenty women who worked at sewing machines along the conveyor belt. It was my job to manage the conveyor belt that sent the women work, and to receive back their completed work. I was responsible for ensuring that they never ran out of work. Each woman was being paid according to how much she was producing. Each woman sewed on a different part of the combat boot and then sent the box of finished parts back to me to be stacked or sent on to another woman to sew on the next part. I had to remember what part of the boot each woman was sewing on.

When they ran out of work, they would turn on the light on a pole that stood several feet above their workstation. When the light lit up on the pole, a corresponding light would come on a panel at my workstation. My job was to get more work to them as soon as possible. The problem was that there would often be several lights on at one time.

When I did not get work to them as soon as they wanted it, they would stand up beside the pole with their hands on their hips and look down the conveyor belt right at me. Every second that they

51

were standing, they were losing money. Whew!! That was a stressful job, but I always kept my "eyes on the prize," knowing that once I entered and completed college, I would have many more job options to choose from.

After I began receiving my checks, my mother and I agreed that I should start buying some of the things I would need for college out of my income. Those were exciting sweet rain days that strengthened my hope that I would really be going to college. Also, it was a fun experience for my mother and I as we picked out some necessary clothing items: a bedspread, rug, sheets and towels, and we stocked up on the personal care items I would need.

By the end of that year of working, my mother and I had saved enough together to pay my tuition for the first semester, buy my books and my meal tickets. I recall that amount being around eight hundred dollars. My plan was to apply for a job through the college Work Assistance Program in hopes that I could earn enough through working and student grants to cover my tuition and other expenses as I moved forward.

After spending a year at my job at *Carolina Shoe Company*, I had a much greater appreciation and praise for my mother, as well as lots of admiration and respect for all the women who worked many years in jobs like this one. College was sounding better and better all the time. I resigned from *Carolina Shoe Company* in early July 1967 to prepare for leaving for my long-awaited college days. I was over the top excited and grateful to be stepping into what I thought would be my wonderful new world, with a wonderful new start to my wonderful new life. I thought, "Yaay!!" I was finally on my way!!!

My consuming desire to escape from my past took over. I was so persuaded by my own thoughts of the new life I anticipated that I went into total denial of my old life that still existed. I told myself that the old me was gone and the new me was waiting in college. I totally denied the reality that I would be taking my old me, my old life with me! The imaginary good news I kept feeding myself was "fake news." The power of "denial" had become so convincing that I decided to give "denial" a feminine name as I was writing this book. I chose the name "Dee" because she was representative of the denial and deception that lived in every bone in my body at that time.

Although my experiences throughout my years in college felt like good news when I shared my financial and academic journey with anyone, and they certainly sounded like good news in the reports I gave to my family and friends back at home, in reality I was promoting fake news because it was coming from a partial, superficial me and not a whole me. The reality was that I was not doing great, I was fooling myself and doing a very good job of it. The old me, and my old life would resurface again years later, but then so would my Jesus!

So, as I packed for college, I made sure to pack all the new things I had bought for my new college life. I had a list that I was checking off so that nothing would be left behind when I departed for Durham. But there were things in my denial state of mind that I thought I was leaving behind forever. That list included four years of sexual abuse and the resulting torment, traumatic pain, a broken heart, the anguish of my father's rejection, the loss of my self-value and identity, and the crushing guilt I felt watching my mothers' pain as my father walked away while I secretly felt glad and relieved to see him go.

I thought I was also leaving the problems of my senior year ordeal with Suede and the white girl behind. Suede received a football scholarship and was on his way to *Fayetteville State College* in Fayetteville, NC. I thought we were both going to have a new start in college and in our relationship. I had built my future expectations concerning college on a fake foundation that would eventually collapse.

The night my father left, I had vowed to myself to make amends to my mother for feeling glad and relieved at his departure. I was twelve-years-old when I made that vow. I had done my best to be the most helpful daughter possible in every way that I could. My mother seemed to have gotten over his departure and she seemed ready to move on. I felt I had tried hard to keep my vow. I felt the bond between my mother and me was strong when I left for college, dismissing the existence of my secret keg hidden deep in the back of my mind.

When I arrived on the *North Carolina College* campus in Durham, N.C., I immediately began feeling a way I had never felt before. I loved the feeling of being independent, being in control of my own life, making my own decisions and being in a totally new environment. The campus was large and very picturesque, with rolling hills, verdant greens, lush plant life and beautifully manicured landscapes. The buildings were all made out of red bricks with tall stately white columns. I immediately felt proud to be there, as I took my first stroll around the campus. The freshman dormitory where I would be living was a newly built, seven-story, sandy colored brick tower. It was perfect for the new life I was beginning in college. My dorm room was located on the seventh floor.

I had come by bus from home to Durham, and by cab to campus, like a surprising number of other freshmen girls. Entering the building, I could smell the odor of new paint, new tile floors and new furnishings. The air was full of energy, excitement and the cheerful chatter of a lobby full of freshmen girls. The hustling, bustling and colliding of a huge number of suitcases and trunks was occurring, and the long line at the elevators increased the level of chatter and excitement in the air. I felt happy, excited and ready for my new life.

The campus was large enough to give you a good walking work out every day to get to classes, but not large enough to need a car if you lived on campus. The campus was located inner city, on the bus line, about a twelve-minute walk to a favorite fried chicken restaurant that the students loved. I was ten minutes from downtown and twenty minutes to a mall by bus. I was set. I felt I had everything I needed to survive and more.

It took me about a week to settle into my dormitory, to start connecting with my first roommate (who never returned after the Christmas holiday), to register for classes, to apply for the Work Assistance Program, to familiarize myself with the campus and neighborhood, and to take my first steps toward joining the NCC College Choir. Once I began my full load of classes and homework, received my part-time work assignment in the campus snack bar, auditioned and began rehearsing with the college choir, and welcomed my second roommate (who remained my roommate throughout the remainder of our years in college), I fell into a groove that left me very little time to think about myself. That worked very well for me.

Compared to other possible work locations on campus, the on-campus College Snack Bar was a fun place to work. A new Student Union building was completed a year later and included an expanded food and dining area that replaced the old Snack Bar. In addition to the new snack bar area, the building also had a large game room with tables and chairs for playing boardgames. It was an area where both on-campus and off-campus students routinely gathered before, between and after their classes. Playing cards became a major activity in the game room area, along with eating. The snack bar stayed busy, and my popularity grew just because I was always there, albeit working mostly.

When I had free time, sometimes I would go over to the game room and play cards. I considered myself a pretty good Bid Whiz and Spades player. There were always older off-campus men mixed in with the on-campus guys hanging out there. Some of the off-campus men were married and looking to make a connection with a younger woman on campus. The girls on campus made a point of spreading the word, letting each other know the game they were running and to beware when spending time in the Student Union. Working in snack bar area, I became familiar with some of them as they came in and out buying food.

I had my share of flirtatious come-on's while at work, from both on and off campus men. I liked the attention, flirted back and kept it moving. Nothing I heard or saw appealed to me. I loved Suede and wanted our relationship to workout. Things between us were going okay and I wanted it to stay that way.

When my college life began to include decisions on whether or not to drink alcohol, smoke Pot or cigarettes, I said, "Yes" to all three and thought, "Why not, everybody's doing it." It was the Sixties and everybody did everything. By my junior year, drinking and smoking Pot were common activities during my weekends. The whole culture in my generation at that time was bent toward living the party life. If you were hurting, you drank something or smoked something or took something and danced it off in a nightclub or at a house party. My social environment and personal habits enabled me to keep "Dee" (denial and deception) as my best friend. It became even easier to accept Dee as my best friend and forget my past when I was under the influence of good Pot, cold beer, *Kool* cigarettes, and a party scene with loud music and partying friends to enjoy it all. Thanks to my job at the college snack bar, I also added food to my survival list.

I began living for Friday nights. My weekday life was jam-packed with study time, deadlines for assignments, writing papers, taking exams, on top of dealing with the demands of work and choir rehearsals. My job at the snack bar was helping to pay my way through college, but it was also setting me up for over eating, which resulted in my considerable weight gain. I had the option of facing the weight problem I was seeing in the mirror, or listening to my best friend Dee.   Dee won out again, and the eating problem lasted for years. Deceived by Dee, I breezed along locked in that gear for all of my college days and well beyond, but my ride with Dee took a hit my junior year in college.

I joined the college choir my sophomore year and it became the only campus organization I would join. I knew from my high school experiences in the choir, and from my earlier experiences singing in the choir at the church with Lace and Satin, that my alto voice could blend well. When I auditioned with the director of the college choir for an alto position, he asked if I would consider singing in the tenor section. He explained that he was lacking tenor voices and he thought mine would be a good fit. I said yes, thinking the tenor ranges might fit my contralto voice even better than alto. During the audition, I discovered that singing tenor fit my voice very well. The ranges were more comfortable for me than singing alto.

I joined rehearsals soon after that and took a seat in the tenor section that was made up of all guys. I liked the idea of being the only girl in the tenor section. I quickly made friends with a couple of guys. My life in the college choir became a source of some sweet rain days. First, I was chosen for the concert choir, and soon after for the touring choir. The touring choir was the top level. The touring choir gave me annual opportunities to travel and perform with the choir throughout the Southeastern United States, and it also provided many sweet rain memories with my fellow choir members.

It was near the end of my junior year in the choir when my devised life with Dee (denial) took a big hit. *(Connie, I'm unclear what the first hit was. Please clarify.)* There was one guy, Polyester, in the tenor section who had taken a romantic interest in me during my sophomore year in the choir. I had no romantic interest in him. I related to him in a friendly manor, mainly because he and I were both members of a group of about eight choir members who had formed a gospel group. We were an independent group who sang occasionally on campus and at churches in the community.

Polyester's interest in me continued to grow, and so, to quell his interest, I decided to tell him that I already had a serious relationship with my high school boyfriend who was attending *Fayetteville State College*. He appeared to take that news well, and casually asked me his name. Without hesitating, I told him Suede's name, and our conversation flowed into another subject.

The conversation never crossed my mind again until I saw him on another occasion a couple weeks later. We started chatting, and unrelated to our conversation, he gave me a girl's name and asked if I had ever heard of her. I said, "No, I don't think so. Does she go to NCC," I asked. He said she goes to Fayetteville State. He went on to say that he had a cousin at Fayetteville State who knew Suede, and his cousin told him that this girl was going with my boyfriend. I was stunned. I went into shock. I froze. He told me my boyfriend's campus nickname and football jersey number, which were correct. He went on to say that he had met the girl himself and that she said that she and Suede were girlfriend and boyfriend.

I don't remember saying anything back to him. I don't remember walking away. I don't remember walking back to my dorm. I believed what I had heard Polyester saying was true. Without any ability to stop myself, my mind immediately transported me back to the pain of the "other girl" scenario from my senior year of high school, and then further back to the intense emotional pain of being abused and rejected by my father.

The pain and insecurities left behind by what my father had done began bubbling up out of the keg in my mind. These old toxic emotions mingled with my fear of rejection left over from the high school girl scenario, and merged with the unexpected onslaught of fresh fears of rejection, insecurities and emotional hurt that came from Polyester, who professed to be a caring friend. I fell apart on the inside. I could find no ability to think my way back to a stable place to endure the onslaught. I felt frantic on the inside and frozen on the outside.

I was overwhelmed by the combined weight of all the painful emotions I was feeling at one time. To be honest, I don't remember the days following my ambush by Polyester. I know I was at least showing up for work and for classes. True or untrue, what Polyester told me never left my mind for days and days. I was fighting again to find a place to stand and a little air to breath as I kept sucking it in and holding down the lid. My beer drinking and Pot smoking escalated and helped with my escape. I was coming back around a little, but it was my anger and a desire to get even that was fueling my come back. I needed some kind of outlet for my anger and my desire to get even.

The only means of communication between Suede and me were the pay phones in the hallways of our dorms. When Suede and I finally talked, I asked him if he had a girlfriend on his campus. He sounded surprised that I asked that question and said he didn't. I asked him if he knew a girl by the name Polyester had given me, and he said he did, but that she was not his girlfriend.

None of it really mattered because I had already made up my mind. I listened to what he said, but I decided I would never trust him again. I decided that my days for trusting any man were over. The one man, my father, who I should have been able to trust and count on, grossly abused me. In my mind, the first and only man I fell completely in love with and wanted to trust had failed to be trustworthy twice.

Whether his side of the stories about either the high school girl or the new girl at Fayetteville State were true or not, it no longer mattered. In my mind, he was guilty of both charges. Polyester, with whom I had no real personal relationship, had ambushed me, obviously hoping to sway my attentions his way by giving me some very toxic and painful information.

I drew a line. I would not keep allowing the men in my personal life to hurt me. My mind, will and emotions made a decision to protect my heart from any further trauma. After doing an assessment of my life regarding men at that point, it became obvious to me that where there was a man in my life, there was going to be pain. I felt I had to protect myself from men or they would destroy me.

I calculated and devised a plan of how I could win the relationship game with the men in my life, or at least break even. I created two rules for my own survival. Rule number one was to never trust a man again and always stay on guard. Number two was to get them before they get me, and then keep it moving. With my two new self-protective survival rules in place, I felt I was ready to move forward.

The next time I saw Polyester, I gave him no indication that his news had affected me so severely. I was ready to play the relationship game now and I intended to win. Secretly, I never wanted to see this guy again as long as I lived. But I did not want to explain anything to all the friends we shared. So, I let it go.

The more I tried to stay away from him, the more he pursued me. He began telling other guys in our gospel group about his feelings for me, and they eventually started mentioning to me what he had told them. I just said I already had a boyfriend. Fortunately, Polyester was in the senior class and was set to graduate a few months later. His graduation day came and it was a day I celebrated too.

But after his graduation, Polyester continued showing up on campus, supposedly to visit friends. I kept trying to dodge him, but he kept coming. It felt like he was stalking me. The next time I saw him, instead of dancing around how I felt, I told him point blank to forget any thoughts he had of being with me. It was my senior year at that point. I told him I would be returning to my hometown along with Suede.

For half a second, I felt a little guilty about how I did that, but I quickly told myself to get over it because he never felt any guilt about the bomb he dropped on me regarding Suede. He only wanted what he wanted. How I would feel never mattered to him. I felt that he was just another man looking to use me for his own selfish gain. At that point, I was sick of being taken advantage of. I was angry and fully focused on revenge. In my mind, I had knocked him down, stepped over him and kept it moving.

With my senior year grades looking pretty good, things going good on the job and my party life buzzing along even better than before, I was heading down the home stretch to graduation. With my best friend Dee (denial and deception) in full swing, I was getting good at keeping myself protected.

Walking out on campus one day, I ran into a man I knew was from off-campus. I also knew he was married. He started with his usual flirtatious opening, gave a few lavish compliments and then slowly proceeded to close with his usual invitation to get together some time. I said, "Okay!" I could tell He was surprised by my flippant response, but he jumped at the opportunity.

I thought the tide had turned. I was doing the manipulating and I planned to use him to even my score with men and to get some secret revenge on Suede. He gave me the details for the secret rendezvous. I met up with him. In my mind, I was just evening up my score and completing my secret plan of revenge on Suede. Both of us got what we wanted. But this time, I thought, I was a winner too. I came away with what I wanted instead of being the loser. I had no idea of the price I had just paid for that "fake" win.

As I was leaving the room, he asked when we could get together again and I turned and answered, "No thanks." After seeing the surprised look on his face, I closed the door and kept it moving. I had crossed the line and didn't even know it. With this act, my disdain and bitterness towards men erupted and began to boil. I felt I was finally on the "dishing it out end," and it felt good! It felt really good!!

This was just the beginning of numerous "fake" wins. I wasn't finished by any means, but thank God, He wasn't finished with me either. I had hit the bottom without knowing it. I didn't know then that He was the God over the bottom places in my life because amazingly, even there, I was still His Girl!!

Yes. He let me hit that bottom and it would not be a short visit, but remember that it says in the Holy Bible that in all things God works for the good of those who love Him, who have been called according to His purpose. At this point in my life, it could only be the supernatural love of God that would be able to rescue me from the grip of bitterness and revenge that had plunged me to these depths. It could only be His amazing grace that would be able to transform me into His usable servant with a purpose. Why would He do this for me when I was so sin stained and fallen? He would do it because He knew somewhere inside me was still a little girl who loved Him. It would take a lot more time to bring her out, but He would do it because I was His Girl!!!

Chapter 5

Slipping into Darkness

Suede and I were both successful in college and graduated in 1971. We were twenty-three years old when we returned to our hometown. He was my first and only real love, and he was my first lover. So far, I have never experienced the sweet rain of being in love or of having a real lover in my life again.

When Suede and I left home for college, I felt like I was a victimized and helpless little girl who had been overwhelmed by the pain inflicted on me by the men in my life, but that was not who I was when I returned. In my mind, I was returning well prepared for any man who would try to deceive me, hurt me or do anything that threatened my sense of security, and that included Suede.

I was actually living a double life, but never admitted it at the time it was happening. I had one life I lived in the world of relationship games with men, and another life that contained my family, friends and professional associates. My secret vow to myself was that I would never allow myself to be hurt by a man again. My helpless victim days were over. It was a new day and as they say, "I had a new attitude." My new strategy for my survival was hidden on the inside of me, inside that terribly crowded keg containing tons of other unprocessed toxic emotions.

My "extreme makeover" on the inside in no way resembled the same old me everyone was seeing from the outside. My family members thought they were welcoming back the same old me because I could be the same old me with them. My life with my Mother, Denim, Lace and Satin was the same. They were not a threat to me, only men were. The family was my eternal sweet rain, and none of them had any idea who I had become on the inside.

My mother and both Lace and Satin were doing well. Denim was still having adventures up North and was doing fine. Lace, who was two years younger than I, had married right after graduating from high school and had gotten a job at *Western Carolina Center*, another state-run local facility. Satin, my youngest sister had followed in my footsteps and was a rising sophomore at *North Carolina College*, which had become *North Carolina Central University*. She was also a member of the College Choir. I hoped with all my heart that her time at NCCU would be filled with sweet rain.

Life had also changed for my mother. While I was in college, she met and married a local man who became a faithful and caring husband to her, and a wonderful Stepfather for the four of us. A lot of sweet rain was falling in the lives of my family members back at home.

As I settled back in at home with my mother and Stepfather, I began to focus on finding employment. There is an old adage that goes, "it's the squeaking wheel that gets the oil." My life really was split into two worlds. There was my world of relationship games with men that utilized a lot of my mental and emotional energy. It was the squeaking wheel that I had to oil all the time.

My other world was much more pleasant and easy going. It was my world of family and friends. Now I was about to add a totally new work and professional life component to that world. I was very excited about finding a meaningful job serving other people. I wanted to find a job that I would love.

Suede had already found a teaching job at one of the local middle schools. I had a good idea that just across town would be the place for me to start looking. I was off to find my first job after graduating college. I was so excited. This world was much better than my other world. As I drove through the downtown area, I passed the old County Courthouse where the museum was housed that contained pieces of my grandfather's history and legacy in Burke County. I was still so proud of him and thought to myself that he would be proud of me for graduating from college.

Coming over the next hill, I saw again with fresh eyes the beauty of my hometown. My hometown was in an area often referred to as "God's Country" because of the natural beauty found there. Morganton is located in the mountains of Western North Carolina, fifty-four miles east of Ashville, N.C. It is a very small town located in the foothills, surrounded by green mountain peaks, rolling green pastures, a gorgeous lake and sparkling streams.

Morganton is still uniquely known for being the location of several large state residential facilities, including the *North Carolina School for the Deaf*, a large Correctional Facility for youthful offenders, *Broughton Hospital*, and Western Carolina Center, which is a long-term residential facility for children and youth who have mild, moderate and severe mental and physical disabilities. After graduation, I had planned to return home and find employment at one of the state facilities.

Western Carolina Center was my first choice. I had earned a Bachelor of Arts Degree in Sociology with a Minor in Therapeutic Recreation. I applied and landed the job. The facility served several types and levels of disabled children. I ended up working a total of fifteen years at WCC, and gained experience working with a variety of children who had mild, moderate and severe disabilities.

My job title was Therapeutic Recreational Specialist and I functioned as part of an Interdisciplinary Team composed of a Medical Doctor, Registered Nurse, Clinical Social Worker, Educational Specialist, Psychologist, Physical Therapist and Occupational Therapist. These teams met weekly to assess and analyze the needs and progress of the patients, and to establish the Care Plans and Goals for each of their residents. Each of the Residential Buildings on campus had its own separate Interdisciplinary Team designed to care for the specific needs of the residents living in the building. It was the Therapeutic Recreation Department Director's job to assign a Recreational Specialists to a Residential Building when an opening occurred on the Interdisciplinary Team in that position.

The Director would normally announce the opening and invite the Specialists interested to let her know. She would select the Specialist. My first assignment after being hired was in a building where young moderately mentally disabled children resided. Over the years I was there, I gained experience working with children at every functioning level and degree of disability.

I loved my job and I loved working with disabled kids. I had found myself a sweet rain job. One day a new opportunity arose at work that I felt I should pursue. It all began at a staff meeting for all the Therapeutic Recreational Specialists. The Director announced an opening in a building that served residents with multiple severe disabilities. I had never worked in that building, but I was familiar with the children who resided there. I knew this was the most emotionally challenging group of children to work with on the campus. This unit was composed of children who had severe multiple disabilities. Most were severely mentally disabled, deaf, blind, non-verbal and non-ambulatory (wheel chair bound). Most were the size and weight of children their age, but they functioned on the level of babies and needed complete care. None of them could talk, but some could make sounds. Some were hydrocephalic (had enlarged heads) and had deformed faces and bodies. For whatever reason, I felt lead to fill that position. There usually was not any competition for working in that building. I told the director I wanted to give it a try and she assigned me right away.

I came on board as the new member of the Interdisciplinary Team in that building. I began spending some time becoming familiar with my residents, doing some assessments and writing my treatment plans and objectives for the residents I would be serving. Therapeutic Recreation options for children with severe mental and physical disabilities, coupled with being blind, deaf and non-verbal were very limited, but not non-existent. Sensory Stimulation was an area that was being used at that time to keep children like these engaged and interactive in their environments as much as possible.

Sensory Stimulation utilizes the senses that the child still has that are functional. With some of these children, those were touch, smell and taste. I created activities and situations to give them opportunities to feel different fabric textures making contact with their skin, and made note of their response.

Water Therapy, or floating them around in the swimming pool seemed enjoyable and relaxing to almost all of them. Presenting them with sniffs of different smells or odors was easy to do, and noting their responses gave me ideas of their likes and dislikes. To investigate some of their taste preferences only required me providing some tasty samples. Ice cream was always the winner. Some knowledge of what they liked or enjoyed could be gained by observing their body language and facial expressions while they were involved in their daily routines. Good eating and sleeping patterns were also indicators of feeling well and contentment.

I think I had been there about a year when I had my bright idea. My idea was to take some of them to the beach. Beach trips were an annual event for a lot of the residents at WCC, but the children in this building had never gone before. It probably never occurred to the staff in the building that children with their multiple disabilities and limitations could benefit from a trip to the beach. I thought they could and at the next Interdisciplinary Team Meeting I presented a proposal for taking them on a weeklong beach trip. The medical doctor on the team immediately responded with, "Not a good idea," based on the medical risk to their health, such as breathing problems, sun exposure, allergy concerns and the tremendous amount of medications that would have to be taken along. He went on to say, if something should happen we would be liable, blah, blah, blah. The Registered Nurse on our team popped up and said she would go and take care of all of that.

At that time, Interdisciplinary Teams were led by a Unit Director, and our Unit Director seemed to be open to the idea. It appeared that some other team members who were not very vocal could go either way. The discussion was scheduled to continue at our next meeting. The RN and I both had taken children in other buildings to the beach. We joined forces to meet any objections that might come up at the next meeting.

The doctor did not hesitate to make his opinions known among the staff in the building. The RN and I were drawing up a list of possible benefits the beach trip could have for the children, when the RN came up with a real game changer. She suggested we inform the parents of the children about the possible trip and see what they might have to say. After those parents got through writing letters and voicing their excitement and strong support for the trip it was a "done deal."

The RN and I worked together to plan every aspect of the trip. We needed about 6 Health Care Technicians to go with us to pull it off and we needed their supervisors to agree and arrange for that many staff to be gone for a week. Everyone supported us. The trip was confirmed, scheduled and our oceanfront beach house was rented. The trip was months away, but most of the staff members were buzzing around and getting excited about our "Unique" Special Needs Children's first-ever beach trip. Those other children on our campus weren't the only ones going to the beach. Our children were going too, and their parents were elated!

The day finally came. We loaded up the bus with six children, six staff, a ton of supplies, clothing and disposable diapers, coolers crammed full of the special foods they would need, their medicines, special medical equipment and our gear. We took off for the beach. After a six-hour drive, we arrived safely. Our week was spent making sure those children had the best time possible. Have you ever tried to push a wheel chair in the sand? Just so you know, you can't.

Imagine you are walking down the beach and come upon six wheelchair- bound children with apparent multiple disabilities, along with six adult men and women of various skin colors buzzing all around them. What would you think? As staff members, it was the most physically challenging and exhausting week of our work lives. But, just like my grandchildren when we go to the beach, those children ate better, slept better and were more relaxed and content that week than any of us had ever seen them before. They were more alert and responsive than we had ever known them to be. They could smell the ocean, feel the sand, feel the breeze and they had all the ice cream they wanted. Based on their responses while at the beach, I believe those children had a week of sweet rain days!! When their parents saw the pictures and heard our reports, they were overwhelmed with joy and very grateful for the rare opportunity their special child had to go to the beach.

When we were going through the process to get the trip for them, I felt like that week was going to end up being one I would probably always remember and it was. It was a week I still feel proud and joyful to have been part of. On the meaningful scale, it got a "ten" from me. It was an experience that felt very satisfying on the inside. It was the first piece in my collection of priceless "over the top sweet rain days.

Back on the other side of town, or should I say in my other world, things were not going so sweet**ly**. For a while, I felt the love Suede and I had for each other, but the time was brief. The incident with the white girl our senior year of high school eroded it for me. What was left was ripped away by the bitter rain typhoon that hit his family our sophomore year of college. He never recovered from it. The high school Suede I fell in love with disappeared and the emotionally wounded Suede took his place.

Like me, he had sucked in his painful family ordeal, pushed it down as deep as it would go, slammed the lid tightly, used the bolts of denial to clamp it down tight**ly,** and kept it moving. The drinking and smoking Pot that we both casually engaged in during our college days became crutches for emotional survival for both of us.

Where my usage had been just an aide, his usage became a dependence that with time became a source of many more bitter rain days in his life.

My love for him was stuffed far down inside me. Watching him go through those bitter rain days stirred the love that was still there. I cared and I tried to be there for him. I tried to be someone he could lean on and trust, but he shut me out. I gave up without any long-term effort. Shutting me out felt like rejection and I could not handle feeling rejected. Now, neither of us trusted each other. Both of us were emotional cripples.

But in spite of the hurt and brokenness we both hid inside, and my denial of the mess my life had become, we were still planning to marry. During the years at home prior to us getting married, our relationship would be best described as a roller coaster ride. There were some ups proceeded by some hair-raising downs and one twisting curve after the other.

Rumors about him and other women were constantly flying around our small town, and his seeming lack of interest in me was causing me to constantly stay in the "never trust him and stay on guard" mode all the time. Break-ups were frequent and at times lengthy, but break-up times became the only time I got a break from the intensity of constantly being in the "stay on-guard" mode.

Break-ups gave me the freedom to go out to nightclubs with my girlfriends. My only intentions were to use the men I would meet to have a good time. I wanted relief from the constant focus on Suede and from the constant stress of staying on-guard. I wanted to use men to make me feel better. The longer our break-up, the more time I had to feel like I was getting even, and to rebound from the stress. My drinking and Pot-smoking remained necessary ingredients for my survival in the world of relationship games, whether I was with Suede or with strangers in clubs. These old habits were also very helpful in maintaining my ability to continue living in denial.

Suede and I ended up marrying at age thirty. Our daughter, Chiffon, who was the sweet rain that filled both our lives, was born when we were thirty-two-years old. Chiffon's birth was the second piece in my collection of priceless "over the top sweet rain days." I will share all of them with you as our road trip continues.

I chose to give birth to Chiffon without an Epidural. I wanted to do natural childbirth. Many women were trying it at that time. I was on board, but Suede was not. I learned the breathing techniques anyway and decided to give it a shot by myself. Suede hung out in the father's waiting room with all the other cowards. My mother and Lace and Satin were there for me, and all of them piled up in my room. I did it!! I had Chiffon without an Epidural, but she weighted in at 6lbs. 4oz., not 10lbs. 4 oz. like me. Would I have done it again? Absolutely not!! After my "No Epidural experience," I felt pain every time I thought about what my mother went through. OH MY GOODNESS!!

From the first moment Suede saw Chiffon, he determined that she became his sweet rain. Our marital life remained more of the same. We were two broken people living separate lives built on denial. At thirty-four, Suede and I legally separated, and at thirty-six we divorced, still holding on tightly to our individual unhealed hurts, unmet needs and unresolved issues. Neither of us made any effort to fight for our own emotional restoration or for our marriage. He was in one corner holding onto his messed-up life and I was in the other corner holding on to mine. When the bell rang, we both walked away.

In my emotional and mental condition at that time, walking away from my marriage to Suede was not that hard to do. I did love him, but I felt I had to love myself more if I wanted to survive. My attention was focused on what I wanted and what I needed and what might happen to me. Walking away was what I saw my father do. Before he walked out, he always looked unhappy and always acted dissatisfied with being with us. Walking away was his solution to his dissatisfaction in his marriage.

Nothing I had seen or heard in my environment indicated that staying in a marriage was a serious commitment to another that was worthwhile or valuable. I did not see walking away as big deal, except for what happened with my mother when my father walked away. I cannot bear to remember the pain of that scene. Seeing my mother's pain that night was the reason I knew I had to get men before they could get me. I saw what walking away could do. Who knew that I would grow up and choose to use that very same selfish and painful solution, over and over again.

When my father walked away, he put into motion a cycle that would negatively impact three of the children he left behind. Unfortunately, divorces became a fairly common occurrence for me and for two of my siblings. Later on, I would come to see divorce as a family curse.

Reconciliation between Suede and me happened years later when he came down for Chiffon's high school graduation here in Atlanta. I told him I was sorry for my part in our marriage not working out, and he admitted his part in it too. Our reconciliation was bittersweet rain for us, but allowed us to have a friendly relationship from that point moving forward. Our reconciliation was all sweet rain for Chiffon. This happened after I had reconnected with *Him*.

After my divorce from Suede, things got even darker. Suede was given court permission to have Chiffon every other weekend. He was a good father to her from day one. I had no problem with him having set times with her, especially since I knew she would actually be staying with his mother at her home. His mother was great with Chiffon, and so was Suede.

But that change allowed me to spend my free weekends bar hopping from town to town. Casual, quick relationships with men became routine. At this point, I had totally convinced myself that not caring about these men gave me an automatic victory over them. I had slipped into darkness and had no idea what was really going on inside me. I felt I was getting my revenge, and it was getting sweeter all the time. Ending the relationships was when the revenge was sweetest because I could show men how little I cared. No matter who ended the relationship, when I walked away, none of them ever heard a word from me again. I knew how to keep it moving.

But I would marry again, not out of love, but out of mutual gain. His name was Corduroy. Although unspoken, we were both playing the "what's in it for me game." When things did not turn out like I wanted and not like he wanted either, things got shaky. Corduroy's emotional and mental situation was almost identical to what I had experienced with Suede. As it turned out, He also had serious unresolved family issues, unhealed hurts, problems with infidelity and a dependence on alcohol. The difference with him was that I was not in love with him and I no longer trusted any man. My guard stayed up and I could see what was coming. I asked him to leave before he could get more out of the deal than I was getting.

My guard was up. I saw it coming. "Get them before they get me," was one of my two survival techniques. Corduroy never had a chance to hurt me because I guarded my heart. The marriage barely lasted three years. I filed for the divorce. I walked out of marriage number two, but there would still be one more marriage. That one comes later in our road trip, after my reconnection with *Him*.

I really had to keep it moving this time. There were two exes and me in Morganton. That was totally unacceptable! I started making plans to move Chiffon and I to Atlanta. For whatever reason, Suede didn't fight me on the move. His life had taken some big hits over the years and he was struggling to make ends meet. He knew I was familiar with Atlanta because he and I had lived there briefly earlier in our marriage. He knew I would be coming back and forth to see my family and that I would never try to take Chiffon away from him. He also knew that Denim lived in Atlanta.

I sold my house, making enough to possibly cover Chiffon and I while I looked for a decent paying job in Atlanta. I got rid of my car, along with the car payment, and found an old turquoise blue Datsun for a few hundred bucks that ended up lasting us a whole lot longer than I expected. That car was like an army tank.

I was hoping to quickly find a good job in Atlanta, and maybe use some of my funds from the sale of the house to kick off my sideline business. My plan was that my new career would start in Atlanta. I definitely wanted a career change. I was done with the jobs in the social services field. I had a new attitude about that too. Social services jobs came with high demands and low salaries. I would need a good income to cover the cost of Chiffon and I living in

Atlanta. Chiffon was six years old when we moved. It was the summer before first grade for her.

My plan was to become an entrepreneur and build my own business. Over the years, there had been a couple of small sideline businesses I started. One was a jewelry business I started during the time period when 10k and 14k gold jewelry had become very popular. I did this for a couple of years until the market cooled off for gold jewelry. When my profits could no longer cover my travel expenses to New York where I was buying the jewelry at wholesale prices, I gave up the business.

My other business was a full-service party planning service that showed good potential in Morganton. My first couple of parties had been successful. Both my client base and the number of parties were looking hopeful when I decided to move. My plan was to pursue the same kind of business in Atlanta as a sideline venture.

Things had changed so much. When I got home after graduating from NCCU at age twenty-three, my heart's desire was to find a meaningful job serving other people. Here I was approaching age forty, and leaving for Atlanta. I could not even feel my heart. All that was there were thoughts of me, me, me! I had been doing the same things over and over, but I never saw the insanity in it. I could feel that secret keg hidden deep inside me boiling, but I was totally absorbed in my own survival and getting even with men.

In my mind, my man-to-man-to-man campaign to hurt men was successful and satisfying. The cost to me was getting lost in the darkness of the bitterness that I had perpetuated. I did not realize that my hatred and bitterness towards men was the flame that was making the keg boil.

With my vow still intact that no man would ever hurt me again, and my survival instinct to trust no man, I set out for Atlanta. Dee's helpful bolts of denial and deception were still holding down the lid on the keg, but they would not be able to hold on much longer. As this "ball of confusion" grew in size, I became my own worst enemy. The entire time I spent driving to Atlanta, with Chiffon sitting safely next to me, I fully convinced myself that I was well able to continue playing the relationship game with men and win.

The drive to Atlanta was about a four-hour, thirty-minute trip from Morganton -- five hours if we stopped to eat. The old turquoise blue Datsun would make it, even though it was burning oil and there was smoke coming from the tail pipe. Oh, and there was that problem with the air conditioning. It hardly ever worked. I know now that my old Sienna sounds pretty good, huh?

I'm so glad that you, my readers, are on my road trip with me. So is God, my Father – *Him*. So just sit back, relax or take a nap like Chiffon, because there will be a WHOLE LOT MORE to see and hear about as soon as we arrive in Atlanta! Whew!! They don't call it

Hotlanta for nothing!! I didn't know my life was about to be transformed, but God did!

Chapter 6

GlenCastle: Who, Me?

I had no idea at the time, but Atlanta would turn out to be *ONE BIG GOD- ORCHESTRATED SET-UP*!! God is sovereign, and He sits high, while we sit low. So He sees the whole picture and puts seemingly unrelated things into place, just to put me when and where I'm supposed to be regardless of my foolish intentions to run from Him.

Yep! For His Girl, He strategically orchestrated the people, places and things HE pleased, for the saving of my wretched soul! Read closely, my readers, because you do not want to miss any of this. Think of your own lives as you see how another chapter in my life unfolded.

This would not be our first time in Atlanta. Suede and I lived in Atlanta for a while after we were married. We both thought that moving to Atlanta was a good idea. We had both found good jobs and things seemed to be better for a brief time. Chiffon was born while we were there.

Eventually, some real-life challenges happened that tested the strength of our relationship, and we failed again. Suede lost his job, and my job was not enough to keep us going. He became very depressed and withdrawn. We decided to return home and try to resume our old state jobs.

That worked for me, but not for Suede. He remained unemployed, depressed and withdrawn. The same old deep-seated problems that we still refused to face went right along with us back to Morganton, and they eventually destroyed our marriage. Chiffon was eighteen months old when we returned to North Carolina.

From the very moment Chiffon and I arrived back in Atlanta, things took off so fast that I had zero time to think about me, myself or I. This would become a good thing later on. I felt the excitement, the freedom and the exhilaration of calling my own shots, just like I did when I first arrived on campus at NCCU, but at a much more accelerated pace. In other words, I had to "hit the ground running."

I had come down during the summer and found us a temporary place to stay. It was a very small basement apartment in an older home owned by a senior lady who was just delightful. She lived upstairs alone, except for a son who was in and out. Chiffon and I had our own private entrance to the basement from the driveway, where we could also park our car. It was all we needed, but still, it turned out to be more than I could afford.

We visited with Denim, who was elated to have us back in Atlanta. Like me, he was also dealing with some marital relationship issues and with having to make some big decisions. We had a lot in common. He looked well and it felt good to hang out with him again.

The first order of business was to get Chiffon enrolled in school. That was a big concern for me, especially since she would be a first grader. After checking out one school that I definitely did not like, I looked at another that looked good, but she had to be put on a waiting list. I needed a good school that was ready to receive her so that I could start job hunting. I found a school! I don't know how I found that school, but it was the perfect school for Chiffon. I was so relieved! It was tucked away in a nice neighborhood out of sight. There was a diversity of students and teachers. It was a straight shot about two miles from where we were living. That was a load off my mind.

Then I began the saga of job hunting. Long story short, I could not believe I found no professional level job anywhere in Metro Atlanta. It was the mid-summer of 1988 and before Internet or WiFi, I think. Regardless, I had no access to tech equipment. All I had was a telephone and the good-old "Want Ads." I was also asking some of the people I met day to day for leads on jobs.

Weeks passed without even one good lead. Our funds were dwindling and our rent was not cheap. I dropped like a hot potato my so-called new attitude about not working a job where I was serving people again. At that point, I would have taken whatever I could get in order to have some money coming in. It was all up to me. Suede was in no position to help financially at that time, so I was on my own.

I kept cruising the "Want Ads" and finally came across something. It was a job with Goodwill Industries. I thought, "That's for me!" I called and was caught off guard when I was told it was an outdoor job working as a Donation Trailer Attendant. First, I thought, "Are you kidding me?" Then quickly coming to my senses, I asked how I could apply.

After scheduling an interview and hanging up the phone, I looked around our small apartment and saw that we needed food again, and the rent was due again. Reality set in, as I convinced myself that at least it paid a little above minimum wage. I love the outdoors and I could smoke all the cigarettes I wanted. The drawback would be that I could only work six hours a day and be able to pick up Chiffon from school on time.

I had seriously underestimated how long our funds would last, and I definitely underestimated how long and difficult it would be to find a good job. One thing for sure, I had to find a more affordable place for us to live. The problem was that our apartment was considered very affordable for the Atlanta area, despite my financial woes.

Well, I landed the job as the Donation Trailer Attendant with Goodwill. I was assigned to a trailer located in the parking lot of the Northlake Mall between Macy's and Sears. I was so glad I did not have to worry about running into anyone I knew. That was a relief.

I really did love being outside and I kept that job through the fall, winter, spring and summer. Watching the seasons begin and end was enjoyable. I used my mountain girl survival skills during the winter. I knew how to dress for cold weather, rain and all in between. I worked alone and had time between drop-offs to read some of the large numbers of books that were always donated. I became interested in reading self-help books. Unknowingly, reading those books was another thing that would pay off later.

I was trying to conserve and stretch the little funds we had left and trying to use the job income to pay the rent and buy food. I began taking the bus to work to save money on gas and wear and tear on the Datsun. I had to schedule work hours around Chiffon's school hours, which kept me from working extended hours or overtime.

I had to find a way to live less expensively until I could find a better job. Reluctantly, I called Denim and asked if we could stay with him for a while. Lovingly, he said yes, but he also let me know he planned to move out of the house he was renting in a couple of months. He needed to reduce his expenses too and was looking for a less expensive place further out of the city. I was thankful for any length of time we might have, and we moved in with him. I frantically looked for a better job so that I could be out of Denim's way at the end of the two months.

With time running out, I found out about a Personal Care Home job opportunity that paid no salary, but provided the live-in manager with a free small basement apartment and the breakfast meal. The apartment did not have a kitchen, which meant I would have to buy lunch for myself somewhere near the job site and buy supper for both of us every evening.

The manager's job was to prepare breakfast each morning for the residents and dispense their morning medications. That free breakfast for Chiffon and I came in handy. I learned how to make a big bowl of oatmeal last me through my shift on the Donation Trailer. I could work during the day and was not required to return until about 6 p.m. to check on the residents and dispense nighttime medications before shutting the house down for the night. The owner would prepare or provide lunch and supper for the residents.

I interviewed with the owner and was selected for the job. Moving Chiffon and I was not too difficult because we only had our personal belongings. All my household and furniture items were in storage back in Morganton. Chiffon and I lovingly said so long to

Denim who also moved out a few months later. Again, a way was made for Chiffon and I.

About six months later, the owner of the Personal Care Home was cited by the City Inspector because the basement area failed to pass some inspection requirements. It was nothing life threatening, but the costly repairs had to be done. The owner explained that she could not afford to make the repairs at that time, but the basement could not be used until it could pass the inspection. I would have to move out within thirty days, which was bad news at a bad time. I was shaken by it. I could see no immediate affordable options for Chiffon and me. Renting anywhere required a month's rent in advance, plus a security deposit in the same amount. It looked like Chiffon and I were on the verge of being homeless, but I never said a word to Chiffon, hoping it would somehow work out.

For the next thirty days, all I could see to do was keep doing my job as manager and continue to go to work at the Donation Trailer.

Then one day, not too long after I got that news, I was waiting at the bus stop when I started a conversation with a woman who was also waiting. I mentioned to her that I needed housing for my daughter and myself, but I was having problems finding anything affordable and safe. She told me about Charis Community Housing and a very special housing program they provided for women with children. She told me she lived in one of their duplexes with her children, and invited me to come by for a visit. I took down her name and address and went by a few days later.

The duplex was attractive and in a safe looking neighborhood in Grant Park. During our visit, she told me more about Charis Community Housing and how I could apply. I called Charis the next day and got information over the phone on what I would need to apply. Then the woman on the other end of the phone added something I thought was unusual for a rental inquiry. She said, "Please bring your resume." I set the appointment for a couple of days later and began gathering the documents required, along with my resume.

It was early October 1989. I was on my way to the appointment and really hoping that I could be selected to live in one of their duplexes. That was all I was hoping for. Their office was in the Grant Park neighborhood within walking distance from their duplexes.

I will always vividly remember the day I went to apply. I was still driving my old 1972 turquoise blue Datsun. I was amazed that it had made it down to Atlanta and back to Morganton a couple times. It was on its last leg now and barely able to pull the steep hill up to their offices. The road was unpaved and very muddy. I was puffing away nervously on a cigarette and wondering what I would do when the car finally broke down.

Nearing the top of the hill, I could see a very old stone building to my right, and to my left farther up another hill, I saw it for the first time. It definitely made an impression. A huge three-story stone castle-looking building with guard towers on each of its four corners stood staring down at me. It was so spooky looking. "What is that and what is it doing in Atlanta," I thought.

I stopped to take a better look and quickly noticed how sad it looked. Its windows and doors were boarded up and resembled sad dark eyes. Weeds had grown up the sides of it. It was surrounded by red mud on every side and especially on the hill that led up to it. It was obvious that this property had not been used for a very long time. The building to my right and the one straight ahead, which was supposed to be their office, did not look any better. I parked the Datsun and headed inside trying to dodge all the mud that seemed to be everywhere on this property.

I entered the door and was greeted. I was instructed to fill out the Charis Community Housing application, which I turned in with my resume. I was seated working on the application packet when a woman came out of an office and asked me to come with her. As I followed her, I could see that the interior parts of this building matched the exterior. I could only describe the entire property as very, very rustic, bordering on primitive.

When I arrived at her desk, she invited me to have a seat. She introduced herself as Nancy Flippen. I mentioned I had not finished the housing application, thinking that would be the starting place, but she began by asking me a series of questions about my resume. She had me tell her about the different positions I had held and she had several questions about my background as a resident manager.

The first time Suede and I lived in Atlanta, I worked for about a year and a half as a live-in Resident Manager at an apartment complex designed for paraplegics, quadriplegics and others who were wheelchair bound. Suede and I were given a free apartment unit to live in, and I received a salary for being the manager. Suede landed a job with the company that owned and managed the apartment complex. Chiffon was born while we were living there and it became her first real home in Atlanta.

I had also added the live-in position as manager of the Personal Care Home to my resume. After answering her questions, she asked me to excuse her for a moment and disappeared behind a partition. When she returned, she gave me information about Charis Community Housing, including a description of the purpose and objective behind the duplexes, which were called *Interim Housing*. She told me that Charis was a "non-profit" organization that primarily built affordable housing in the Grant Park community for low-income families. That's me, I thought!

She went on to say that Charis and a few other smaller ministries who had offices in the building functioned under the 501 c3 non-profit status of FCS Urban Ministries (known today as Focused

Community Strategies). Charis and FCS were made up of predominantly white staff and volunteers. She said, FCS Urban Ministries had recently purchased this twenty-acre site containing three buildings (the ones I saw coming in), with plans of making Charis the Property Management company for the complex.

The site had been designated as an Historical Landmark by the Atlanta Historical Society. Changes to the outsides of the buildings were not allowed because of this designation, but interior renovations in the buildings, on the grounds, roads and parking lot were to begin soon. The castle looking building up on the hill had been named GlenCastle, and the entire complex would take on that name. The property was located within walking distance of the Georgia State Capitol Building and downtown Atlanta.

GlenCastle had originally been built as The Atlanta Stockade, which was a debtors prison built in the late 1880's. People who could not pay off their debts were jailed in the stockade and made to work off the debt through physical labor. Entire families, including parents and children were jailed in the stockade until they worked off their debt.

The castle looking building was the actual jail, which explained the guard towers located on each corner of the building. The three-story building located down the hill from GlenCastle was originally the blacksmith shop where the men were sent during the day to forge irons. The one-story flat-topped building, which housed FCS-

UM and Charis administrative offices, was originally the stables where the women and children were sent to work tending the animals. They also worked in a garden area.

People were usually not jailed there for long periods of time, but rather long enough to work off the debt they owed. Once the debt was worked off, they were released, but unfortunately many returned when their debt mounted up again. There were no separate cells or divisions for women and men. Everyone was congregated in one area, including the families with children. Conditions were unsanitary and treatment was said to be harsh. She explained that FCS and Charis were Christian organizations that had jointly embraced the vision to see GlenCastle transformed into affordable housing for special needs populations such as the working poor, the homeless, ex-offenders, recovering addicts, senior and elderly aged people, single mothers with children, married couples with children who were homeless, and people with disabilities.

To my total surprise, the vision I was hearing about serving people was capturing me. I was drawn to it. It was very encouraging to hear that a non-government organization was actively pursuing meaningful solutions for people with special needs. It was so encouraging to know that there were people who cared and were putting it into action, just because they cared. That made a big impression on me.

What was even more exciting to hear was that the passion that FCS and Charis had for seeing GlenCastle transformed had caught fire all over Atlanta, and ten of the largest construction companies in Atlanta had agreed to unite in a joint effort to donate labor and materials for renovating the buildings and grounds at GlenCastle. They called themselves GlenCastle Constructors, Inc., and this whole scenario was mega amazing to me.

She said they were looking for a Resident Manager for the special needs people at GlenCastle, and I might be a good candidate. It would be a live-in position that provided an apartment and a salary. I could not believe my ears! I was actually interviewing for a job that could solve my income and my housing problems. Also, there was still a spark of passion left inside me for helping people and doing meaningful work. I was drawn to their vision, encouraged by the huge community support they were receiving and excited about the opportunity to help people in some very meaningful ways. I was excited -- very excited!

But a lot of my excitement turned to worry when I remembered she had said they were a Christian organization, and I definitely was not a Christian. I decided to try not to worry and "just go for it."

Nevertheless, over the next couple days I began thinking about the "Christian thing." I remembered my Grandaddy, who was a Christian. Any time I was at his house at night after he had watched the news, he would go to his room. I would peek in and see him sitting in his chair reading his *Bible*. He had an old Gooseneck Lamp on his night stand that he bent so the light would fall on his *Bible*. In my kid's mind, it seemed like he spent an eternity reading it. I can still picture him now. Those two things were his nightly routines -- watch the news and read his *Bible*.

My mother was also a Christian and she kept us involved in church and Sunday school. There was a time as a child about age five or six when I loved going to Sunday School with my friends on the street. I felt good being in church, especially in Sunday School. My favorite songs were *Jesus Loves Me, He's Got the Whole World in His Hands* and *This Little Light of Mine*.

When the sexual abuse started, I became very confused. I had learned in Sunday School that Jesus loved me and was watching over me. So, I prayed and prayed asking Jesus to help me. I asked Jesus to stop my father from abusing me. The abuse continued. I stopped asking and I stopped believing Jesus loved me. I walked away from Jesus at eight-years-old, feeling abandoned by Him. I felt lost and totally alone.

I kept going to church because my mother expected me to go. When I got old enough to make my own decisions about going to church, I turned my back on church and on Jesus. Over the years, I would attend church services sometimes going along with my family members. Lace and Satin gave their lives to Christ as young adults. They were active in their faith and in their churches.

There were a couple of occasions where I could have been seen heading down a church isle at an altar call or prayer call, but they were only a response to feeling convicted and guilty. The trips to the altar made me feel better momentarily, but nothing ever changed. My heart had turned to stone. I had walked away from Jesus, just like I walked away from my marriages. None of my exes came after me, but Jesus did.

Interview day came. I put on the grey wool suit and white blouse I had gotten from the Goodwill Store, thinking I looked professional and conservative, but I was not feeling confident at all. I kept thinking, what if they ask me questions about my faith or ask if I was a Christian. I forced those thoughts out of my mind and tried to replace them with my strengths. It was my resume that had impressed her. I had experience with all types of special needs people, and they wanted a Resident Manager who was experienced in living among the people they would serve. Maybe that would be enough.

When I nervously stepped into the interview room, I was shocked. I was not expecting to see so many people. I was going to be interviewed by a whole committee of White Christians. I almost froze, my heart sank, but I made it to the one empty seat left at the table for me. I was totally out of my comfort zone, surrounded by these people. They had to feel my discomfort and see the stressed-out look on my face as I tried to answer their questions while fearing one about my faith could pop up at any moment. For some reason unknown to me, none popped up, and a few days later, they offered me the job.

I accepted gratefully!! Whew!! I was pleased and relieved to have a good job and a safe place to live for Chiffon and me. I was given the first choice of all the apartment units in GlenCastle! I got to choose any unit I wanted. I chose a third-floor corner unit with a guard tower and several large windows. The guard towers were converted into a small bedroom area. From my kitchen window, I could see the sunrise in the morning, and from my living room window, I could see the sunset in the evening as well as a great view of the downtown Atlanta skyline. I didn't know why all these good things were happening to me. My thoughts were, why me?

When I explained my housing situation regarding moving out of the basement apartment to the Charis Director, she arranged for Chiffon and I to move into one of the duplexes until the GlenCastle renovations were complete. In exchange for living in the duplex, she asked me to start coming into the office, later on, to begin helping with the resident selection process. I told her how grateful I was and how relieved I felt. I told her what this opportunity meant to Chiffon and me.

With these fantastic new occurrences, I felt like a ton of weight had been lifted off me. I called Denim to let him know what had happened, and he was almost as surprised and relieved to hear this good news as I was.

Everything about GlenCastle was amazing to me. Like all of the people involved in the project, I became captivated by the vision. I was filled with the hope that GlenCastle would be a refueling station where new beginnings and new ways of life would take hold and transform the lives of the individuals and families that were coming.

I did not know that Chiffon and I were the first of those families. I did not know that my transformation had already begun. I did not understand why or how all these good things were happening to us since we found this place called GlenCastle. I did not know that GlenCastle would be the place where *HE* would rescue me from myself. But let's get back to our wonderful temporary home in the duplex.

It was now around December 1989. The Opening Ceremony for GlenCastle was scheduled for April 1990. The renovations on GlenCastle had already begun. Chiffon and I had settled in our fully furnished, three-bedroom duplex. Things had settled down even more with it being the holiday season.

For the first time since we arrived in Atlanta, I had time to think about something other than how Chiffon and I were going to survive. Things had slowed down to where I got a chance to think about other things. The first thing I noticed was that the intense stress level I had been experiencing had significantly decreased. The next thing I noticed was that I felt physically exhausted. That led me to remember that my fortieth birthday had come and gone almost unnoticed. I thought, no wonder I felt exhausted, I was old.

I could not believe that more than a year had passed since we left Morganton. As my mind took in that fact, I realized that I had not been club-hopping, drinking, or smoking pot during that time. That world had gotten lost in the background of the immediate needs of my daily life with Chiffon. There had been one brief encounter with a man I met running at the track while living at the Personal Care Home. Other than him, I had not played the relationship game with a man since Morganton.

For the first time, I started taking a look at my world of relationship games with men. Of course, I had never looked at what I was doing. In that world, I only saw myself as protecting and defending myself from all sorts of pain that every man I met would aim at me.

For a minute, I pictured that world in my mind. I could see what that world looked like and feel what it felt like to always be on guard and ready to get them before they got me. I could see what the men looked like, but I could not picture who I am. That bothered me, so I let that thought go and switched my thoughts back to how exhausted I felt.

I did not understand why I was even thinking about that world. It had been a year since a nightclub, drinking, pot-smoking, or getting revenge. I had spent a year without the other world. For the first time, I had spent an entire year absorbed in taking care of Chiffon and providing for our needs.

I felt like turning forty had set off some internal alarm. Is it just me, or is there a reckoning point on forty age? For me, it was my fortieth birthday when I first began to question how I had lived my life to that point. I thought about some of the things I had read in those self-help books when I worked on the Goodwill Donation Trailer.

I realized that my life had suddenly shifted in a positive direction, but I could not explain why. It was nothing I had done. It seemed to be happening on its own, and it seemed to have begun when I arrived in Atlanta. Let's get back to the office at GlenCastle and see how things are developing.

It was mid-February 1990, a few weeks before the building was scheduled to be completed. I was informed that Larnelle Harris, a well-known African American gospel singer, had written a special theme song for GlenCastle. I was told that he would be coming for a two-day visit to record and video the music in the building.

I had never heard of him, but he was well known based on all the excitement and preparation. The building was not open yet, but I had opened the manager's office to begin interviews and resident selections.

Mr. Harris arrived along with his recording team. It was exhilarating to hang out with him and his team and watch the recording. The theme song he wrote for GlenCastle is phenomenal and is still very relevant today. Here are the two verses and the chorus. He titled it "Castle of Hope."

To this old debtor's prison, men were brought to waste away, and their only crime was the debts they could not pay. But the cycle has been broken; all its prisoners set free, now it proudly stands for another chance at life and dignity.

There's a light in every window, and it's doors are open wide. We can feel the hope that has found its way inside. Yet the task is still unfinished, there is still so much to do, but the change must start deep within the hearts of men like me and you.

Chorus: It's a Castle of Hope, it's a bridge to a dream, it's uncommon love for all who dare believe, there is a joy from above as we establish God's love so that all of the worlds can see what caring is meant to be, what caring is meant to be. Written by Larnelle Harris

Today, Mr. Harris is still a prominent gospel singer and songwriter. I did my research on him. He has recorded 18 albums, won 5 Grammy Awards and 11 Dove Awards, and has had several numbers one songs on the inspirational music charts.

Mr. Harris and his team were relentless in perfecting everything concerning the theme song's video. The passion he brought to the effort was evident in his voice and in the words he had created to communicate the vision and mission of GlenCastle.

Mr. Harris didn't know that the first prisoner to be set free had already arrived. He didn't know that my nightmarish cycle would be broken. Mr. Harris didn't know that his song about GlenCastle was a song about me. Mr. Harris didn't know that a change had started deep within my heart, and neither did I.

My focus and passion for helping and serving people would eventually lead me to the truth of how desperately I needed help. God had set me up! Beginning from my birth and throughout my life, His plans for me had been perfectly ordered for my feet to follow His path to my Castle of Hope, GlenCastle.

He had been with me from my beginning and every moment of my life had a place of meaning and purpose.....the good, the bad, and the ugly. It would still take me a long time, say at least ten more years, before I would *fully recognize Him* in my life.

There would be some steps forward and some backward. There would still be some good choices and some bad ones. There would still be some bitter rain and some sweet rain, but *the process* of *my awakening to Him* had already begun. It began the day I crossed the Georgia State Line and came to Atlanta.

God planted that lady at the bus stop, which led to my first trip up the hill to GlenCastle in my old turquoise blue Datsun. GlenCastle was *His* chosen place for my transformation. Now let's go back to where I left off in the office at GlenCastle.

I felt equipped for most of the job but did not know how to manage one unexpected aspect. In the interview, I found out that the Resident Manager would also serve as the Spiritual Coordinator for the apartment community. I thought, Who Me? Me, a Spiritual Coordinator? Now that would be a real problem.

I put that problem on the back burner as I got consumed in learning the property management computer systems, finding suitable applicants, managing the application process, interviewing applicants, making resident selections, moving in residents, and acclimating the new residents.

Finally, all the inside renovations were complete. The grounds and parking lot were just about finished. Beautiful trees, shrubs, and flowers were planted all around the outside of the building. GlenCastle was beautiful inside and out. There were 64 fully furnished apartment units spread out over the three floors and with an elevator. The common areas inside the building included; an entrance hall with marble floors and sky lighting, a resident's lounge, a Coin Operated Laundromat, a Snack Bar with vending machines and tables and chairs, a large front porch that would soon have big white rocking chairs and a side porch equipped with a big barbeque grill and a picnic table.

Another stage of the renovations was scheduled to begin later on at the Blacksmith Shop building. When finished, the three-story Blacksmith Shop building would house a Chapel for Sunday morning services for the GlenCastle residents. There would also be a fully equipped professional kitchen where residents could be trained as chefs, a computer lab equipped with computers, several classrooms, and meeting spaces.

A small amount of interior work had begun on the Stables building, which would remain the administrative offices for FCS Urban Ministries, Charis Community housing, and a diverse array of other smaller ministries functioning under the present-day, Focused Community Strategies organization.

With the GlenCastle building renovations completed, the organizations' focus shifted to preparing for the Grand Opening Celebration. I was gradually learning the job and trying to keep up. Still, the reality of what I had gotten myself into did not fully hit until I received a call from my boss, Nancy Flippen, about the opening celebration. She was excited as she gave me the details of what was being planned.

They had chosen to have a sunrise service on Easter Sunday morning in the front parking lot of GlenCastle. It was going to be a big deal. The GlenCastle Project had been nominated for President George H. W. Bush's 21st Point of Light Award. The GlenCastle story was getting out around Atlanta, and many people were following and supporting the project. The partners of GlenCastle Constructors, Inc. were invited to be there. She said that Atlanta Mayor Maynard Jackson, the FCS-UM Founder, and President Robert (Bob) Lupton and Rennie Scott, the visionary behind the GlenCastle Project, would be on the program.

Then she dropped the bomb. The planning committee wanted me to also be on the program, and they wanted me to do the Opening Prayer. Who Me? I thought. I could have fainted. After a few seconds, I heard myself say, okay...alright. From that moment on, I heard nothing else she said. I could only hear my mind saying, "it's all over now." I was so afraid. I had nothing to draw from...nothing.

I had never seriously thought about praying. I had never really prayed, and now my first try would be in front of an audience of possibly hundreds of prominent Christian people and dignitaries.

The event was about a month away. Gripping fear set in on me that moment and remained until the afternoon after the event was over. My only hope was to write a prayer and read it as far as I could see.

The day came, and I was seated up front on the platform right beside Mayor Maynard Jackson and next to the FCS President,

Robert Lupton, and the visionary for the project, Rennie Scott. I knew why they were all there, but I had no idea why I was there. From my point of view, there was something very wrong with this picture.

When it was time for the Opening Prayer, I stood, walked to the podium, and read my opening prayer verbatim, too afraid to try anything more daring. I felt sure that every Christian on our staff was disappointed that I read the prayer. I know I was. But, no one ever mentioned a word about it. I was still feeling very uncomfortable but very relieved the prayer assignment was at least done. I still couldn't shake the feeling that I wished I could have done a better job with the prayer.

Meeting and greeting people afterward was difficult for me, but the joy and excitement of completing GlenCastle were flowing. Touring people through the building made my interactions with people more comfortable. I still felt out of my comfort zone and so far from being the person they would have wanted for the job.

I did not understand why or how I became a part of the GlenCastle story, but good things were happening despite my feeling that I did not deserve them. I recovered from the grand opening and was back into the office routine, which had become my comfort zone.

A few weeks later, I was working at my desk, enjoying a cigarette, when the phone rang. It was Bob Lupton, the founder and President of FCS. He sounded very cheerful and excited. He told me that the GlenCastle project had been chosen to receive the 21st Point of Light Award from President George H. W. Bush. I got excited, too, until he dropped his bomb.

He said President Bush would be coming to Atlanta to Dobbins Air Force Base to present the award personally, and I had been chosen to go out to Dobbins and receive it on behalf of the organization.

Who Me? I said. I was stunned and totally confused. My responses were a combination of "What did you say…..you should be going…someone else should be sent…..not me….I haven't done anything for GlenCastle….there were so many people that deserve that honor….I don't. He cheerfully stopped me and replied, "we decided that you should go and receive the award…we chose you".

The day came. I went. I met President George H. W. Bush and received the 21st Point of Light Award on behalf of the GlenCastle project. Meeting the United States president was extremely exciting for me, as you would quickly see from the photo taken. I looked more like I was in shock than anything else.

I continued to feel an abundance of uneasiness about the whole thing. I never deserved that honor and did not understand why I had been chosen to have that experience when so many others had worked long and hard for the GlenCastle Project. I had only been there a few months. To this day, I still don't understand why God did that, but *He* did.

I was back in the office, and things were settling back down when I remembered the dreaded part of my job description…..the Spiritual Coordinator. Being the Spiritual Coordinator for the building was a significant part of my role as Resident Manager. The Spiritual Coordinator was responsible for providing events that would help build community among the residents and encourage their spiritual growth. Spiritually, I brought nothing to the table. I was a spiritual zero.

I knew how to "build community" among the residents, so I first started with that effort. I began planning a few community events. The first community event was a Paint Party where all the residents were invited down to the front porch to help paint our ten new rocking chairs. I could handle that, and with the help of several of the residents and their children, some hot cocoa, hot coffee, and Crispy Crème Donuts, that early morning event was a success. All of the rockers had a thick coat of white paint and looked great on our front porch.

I knew I would be safe staying on the community building side, but on the inside, I was bothered by not fulfilling the spiritual role as well. I did not know what to do. Lacking a spiritual life of my own,

I had nothing to draw from. So, I procrastinated and did another community event and then another. I thought, at least I was building community among the residents.

The guilty feeling was still there, and I could feel it. I lived with it until something very unusual happened. A couple of months later, I was sitting at my desk enjoying a cigarette when a petite white-haired, sixtyish looking white woman came bouncing into my office and said, " I am Rev. Nola Love, and I was driving down Glenwood Avenue, when God said, "Nola, turn left right here, you are needed up on the hill. So here I am, how can I help you? ". Yes. This is precisely how it happened.

Immediately, I thought, she can help me with this Spiritual Coordinator thing!! I asked her to have a seat, and I put out my cigarette. I asked her to repeat what she had said again. I had heard her correctly, and I believed she could help me. I needed any help I could find with that component of the job. I filled her in on GlenCastle, and I told her that I was also the Spiritual Coordinator for the community, but I did not know how to do it.

She told me what I needed to do first was to form a Spiritual Committee. I needed to find a few residents who wanted to serve on the committee. She said the committee should pray together and ask God to show us what to do.

I also told her about the Chapel plans and that we would need a minister to conduct Sunday morning services when it was completed. She agreed to assist us with that need and later became our first Sunday morning minister at the Chapel.

Rev. Love went on to provide and sustain a Sunday Morning Worship Service and Sunday School Class for the GlenCastle residents for several years. She also became a constant source of spiritual guidance for me personally. Today, I am still grateful that God told her to turn left up the hill because she was needed indeed!

Shortly after that day, I did what Rev. Love told me to do. I turned my attention to assembling a Spiritual Committee. My most community-minded residents were the band of recovering addicts who spent time interacting together in the building. I began with one particular couple, the Stewart's, who were both in recovery and had two children. I remembered two other men in recovery who showed some leadership skills and seemed to influence the residents. All four of them appeared stable and reliable. When I made my request, they all responded positively and seemed excited to be asked to join the committee.

I will never forget our first meeting. We had a meeting room on the third floor of the building. Three of them showed up. The four of us arrived and chatted for a few minutes in the meeting. I asked them to join me in forming a circle. We all stood and joined hands. I told them what Rev. Love had said about starting with a prayer, asking God to show us where to begin. I then asked who knew how to pray so we could start.

The four of us were standing there holding hands facing each other in a circle, and there was nothing but silence. We were all looking around at each other. I asked again, looking around the circle to see if anyone knew how to pray. I admitted first that I didn't, and each of them acknowledged that they did not either. I said, "Well, the Spiritual Committee is off to a great start," and all of us burst out laughing loudly.

It took a few minutes to pull ourselves back together. Then I suggested that each of us just say what we think we need to ask God in prayer. I started first, but I don't remember precisely what any of us said. I do remember that everything was spoken sincerely.

I forgot our exact words, but I will always remember the bond established that night by our shared lack of spiritual abilities and inexperience. It was hilarious then and now. When I think back on the GlenCastle Spiritual Committee's first meeting, a smile comes right afterward.

A few more residents joined the committee as time passed. These committee members became the pioneers of the spiritual life that developed at GlenCastle and later at our Chapel. We went on to plan and carry out many worthwhile and enjoyable events for the residents. My favorite event became our Christmas Cantata, which was done two different years. We titled it "Emanuel," which means "God with Us."

The residents worked on it for weeks using their resources, talents, abilities, and a lot of their free time. It was an indoor enactment of the Night of Christ birth that I duplicated from my childhood memories. Every Christmas at our little Presbyterian Church back at home in Morganton, Mrs. Davis, our church pianist, would have the neighborhood children do the enactment of Christ's birth. It wasn't officially Christmas until the children did the Christmas Cantata.

The Spiritual Committee and GlenCastle residents created the production complete with authentic-looking costumes, stage props, and a scenic cardboard background. The caste and choir were composed of residents from the building. The narrator was a recovering alcoholic. Mary was a recovering addict. Joseph was a ministry intern who lived in the building while serving GlenCastle as an intern.

The shepherds were men in recovery except for one shepherd, a young white man who had a mild mental disability. Most of the angels were young girls, including Chiffon. But one angel was a young white woman who spent hours of her free time volunteering with the children in the building on the weekends.

One soloist in the choir was a resident who had been convicted of murder as a young man. He had served his time and was released after spending almost thirty years in prison. If I remember correctly, he sang Oh Holy Night and received a standing ovation.

Because of the make-up of our team of residents, the hard work and the time required, the harmony that was prevalent throughout the preparations, and the quality of the finished product, the "Emanuel Cantata" became another piece in my collection of priceless "over the top sweet rain days."

The cantata was well attended by the other residents in the building, by staff members from Charis Community Housing, by Charis and FCS Executive Board Members, by people from the small ministries under FCS- Urban Ministries, as well as people from the surrounding community. The evening also included an excellent reception for everyone! That evening we were all very proud to be on the Spiritual Committee and be a part of the GlenCastle family. God did that!!

Chapter 7

GlenCastle
Pt. 2: U-Turn

Once the Spiritual Committee got its start and became more productive, it sparked more changes in my personal spiritual life. What happened next might be better described as an internal earthquake. It was unexpected. My secret keg and my deep state of denial took a huge hit that night, but it was what God knew I needed to begin my U-turn back to Him.

It happened one evening at home in our apartment in GlenCastle about a year after we got there. Chiffon was visiting at the apartment of a friend she had made in the building. She and three other little girls of her age had become playmates. One of the little girls, I will give the name Velvet because she and Chiffon became best friends. Velvet became like a family member, and she and Chiffon remain best friends today.

I was in the bathroom doing my hair and make-up to attend some outing or event. I was looking in the mirror, arranging my hair, and putting on lipstick. At that moment, I heard, "Look in her eyes." I couldn't. I realized that evening that I could style the woman in the mirror's hair and put on her lipstick, but I could not make eye contact with her. I tried again to look into her eyes, but I could not. That was a breaking point for me. I broke into tears. I emotionally fell apart. I felt so much pain, guilt, and loss. I felt divided as if there were two of me. I felt lost, and I knew she was too.

I knew then that the eyes in the mirror that I could not look into were the eyes of the "little girl inside me" who was sexually molested. I could not look into her eyes because she was hurting, blameless, pure, and innocent, and I was drowning in sinful behavior, guilt, shame, and filled with evil and hateful desires to hurt men and to get revenge.

So much changed during those minutes. I knew then why I could not see what I looked like in my world of men and games that day in the duplex. The me that was once me no longer existed. She had been gobbled up by bitterness, anger, and revenge. The bitter rain poured down on me that night, and all I could do was bow my head to it because I was the source of my bitter rain at that time.

Even in that broken moral state, I still was not ready to face myself spiritually. I chose to blame my father for what he did to me and for what he did to my mother. My father had inflicted double

119

pain on me by treating my mother the way he did that night when he walked away. That night added to what I had endured by his hands for four years; it was too much for me.

I remembered my desperate prayers asking Jesus to do something to keep my father away from me. No help came. I felt I was alone and helpless as the abuse continued. Where was Jesus when the "little girl me" needed Him? Where was He when my mother needed Him? I was furious at my father, and I was very angry at Jesus. I lost trust in men. I felt I could not trust any man. Jesus was included, but He knew it, and He had a plan. He always has a plan!

So, what was happening with my secret keg? It was boiling when I left Morganton to come to Atlanta. Why didn't it blow the evening of the internal earthquake caused by the mirror scenario? I don't know. From what I can see looking back on all of this, it was not God's plan for my keg to emotionally explode all at once because it could have quickly happened that evening. God could have released the full-quota of what I deserved that evening, and I would have emotionally fallen into a thousand broken little pieces, but He didn't.

Instead of an explosion, I began to see that God strategically choose when and how specific bolts on the keg would be loosened, and certain other bolts on the keg would be removed along my journey until all the pressure in the keg was released and dispelled. But as I said before, it would be a lengthy process to gradually release the stress of the bitterness, anger, and desire for revenge that I had succumbed to for three decades of my life. I had a long way to go, but God had a plan for all of it to be addressed.

First, the keg stopped boiling once the flames created by the bitterness, anger, and revenge died down. That happened when we moved to Atlanta, where I spent my first year away from my world of relationship games with men. Being immersed in my world with Chiffon and continually staying focused on meeting our needs left zero time for thinking about me, myself, and I.

My move to Atlanta removed a primary bolt from the keg because my anger and desire for revenge had escalated after the second divorce. The divorce kept the keg boiling the last several months while I was still in Morganton. After the passing of that first year in Atlanta, the flames subsided, but the problems that fueled the fire were still there.

I could also see those unexplainable; right on time, good things showed up when we first arrived in Atlanta like finding that perfect school for Chiffon, the income benefits, and how I enjoyed the job working outdoors on the Donation Trailer and reading the self-help books.

I saw how the housing with Denim happened just when I needed it and the accommodation and small benefits at the Personal Care Home that popped up only when I had run out of options. None of these were just coincidences, and deep inside, I knew it. All of these good things were provided by God to loosen the bolts on my secret keg. I felt the effects of what He was doing, but I was a long way from embracing Him. It felt like He was caring for me and pursuing me, but I wasn't convinced at all at that point. How much patience does God have? A lot, when you are His Girl.

God also used a series of wake-up calls that turned into bolt looseners. Turning forty and realizing how much time had quickly passed by was a wake-up call that got my attention. Things that felt threatening, like picturing my world of games with men and not seeing what I looked like in the picture, became a wake-up call for me. It resulted in me giving some thought to why I could not see myself.

My fear of the Charis Community Housing interview, because I wasn't a Christian, was also a wake-up call that made me think about my past life. It made me revisit the place in my childhood when I felt connected to Jesus. It prompted me to remember how important it was to my Granddaddy to study his Bible and retain the kind of man he was. These wake-up calls were all bolt looseners that provided a release of the pressure inside the keg.

Good things were happening to us, and they had nothing to do with me. I knew I was deserving of nothing good. Still, despite that fact, I had found myself in the company of Larnelle Harris, Robert

Lupton, Mayor Maynard Jackson, and President George H.W. Bush, all within a few months of arriving at GlenCastle.

I could not deny that despite my unworthiness, undeserved blessings were coming my way. I could see the sweet rain falling into my messed-up life, but I had no explanation of why. Little by little, I began thinking that it looked like Jesus might care about me. I could handle a little thinking that way, but I was still a long way from allowing myself to feel that way. It was just too great an emotional risk.

The GlenCastle job requirements, including a Spiritual Coordinator role for the community, should have been a dead give-away of what God had lined up for me. What a shake-up it caused in my spiritual life, and Rev. Love became the perfect spiritual guide for me. Rev. Love and the Spiritual Committee were primary tools God used to remove bolts from the keg. What a set-up that was!

The most awakening experience of all was the showdown in the mirror, the internal earthquake. Another direct bolt was removed from the keg because it pushed me to do something about my broken condition. God set me up again because He knew me, and He knew exactly how I would respond.

Despite my determination to hold on to my vendetta against Jesus and hold on to my bitterness towards my father and all men, I could see these good things happening that God was calling forth into my life. There was no other way to explain them. They were so evident and meaningful that they could not be ignored. God's kindness and attention to my needs were beginning to affect my heart of stone positively.

Aware of my continuing resistance to Him and my resistance to going to church, Jesus used another door for me to begin my U-turn back to Him. The whole time I thought I was in control, He was in control. He knew me well.

I decided to join Al-Anon. I thought it was all my idea. I had learned about Al-Anon from some of the residents who were recovering addicts and alcoholics who were members of 12-Step Recovery Programs. All of the residents in recovery from substance abuse were members of either Narcotics Anonymous or Alcoholics Anonymous. Membership and active participation in a 12- Step Recovery Program was a mandatory requirement for former substance abusers living at GlenCastle.

My father was an alcoholic, and I believed that he was the root of my problems, and I believed that he was to blame for my messed-up life. One theory suggests that girls who have fathers like mine often unconsciously choose men like their fathers. This may have been partially true of me, but my reality was that I wanted to hurt men like my father, who hurt my mother and me.

Al-Anon is a 12-Step Recovery Program for family members and friends of alcoholics. Al-Anon is open to people of all faiths and males and females. Al-Anon refers to all faith sources as a "higher power," whether the "higher power" is called God, Jesus, Allah, Buddha, or something else. However, you are not allowed to discuss your faith source in the meetings.

Step # 1 of the Al-Anon program is *we admitted we were powerless over alcohol (the alcoholic) and that our lives had become unmanageable.* In the case of a family member or friend, it would be admitting you are powerless over the alcoholic and that your life had become unmanageable. Step # 2 is *we came to believe that a Power greater than ourselves could restore us to sanity.* Step # 3 is *we decided to turn our will and our lives over to the care of God as we understood Him.* It can take a long time for new members to process through the first three steps. There are 12 steps in all. The first three took me a while, as well as some of the other steps.

Each member moves through the steps at their own pace. If a member chooses, they can seek a woman in the group to become their Sponsor. A Sponsor is a type of mentor who keeps you on track and accountable. Each member works through each step until they are satisfied and at peace with their outcomes and rely on her Sponsor's feedback. (If you are interested, the 12 Steps of Al-Anon and other information can be found quickly by Googling 12 Steps of Al-Anon).

I took the steps seriously, and it took years to work through all twelve. The first three steps were hard for me, which is relatively common for new members because they require renewing your thinking. But, Step # 4, which is *made a searching and fearless moral inventory of ourselves,* took it to a whole new level, as you can imagine. I put off working on this step as long as I could. It took a lot of firm coaching from one of my mentors for me to address it.

Ugh!! Step # 4 was hard!! I realized how serious I was about changing my personal life when I began working on that step. But I hung in there until I found a place of peace with myself, and my mentors became satisfied with my progress.

Step # 8, *made a list of all persons we had harmed and became willing to make amends to them* led me to reconcile my relationship with Suede. My apology to him helped heal my emotions and freed Chiffon to have the best relationship possible with her father. Because he held on to his *bitter rain days* to the end, she became the only person in his life that he could trust enough to give his love freely. He freely loved Chiffon, and she loved him. It was a constant joy for me to see that exchange.

I stayed in Al-Anon for eight years. God used Al-Anon in many unique ways!!! Al-Anon became an integral part of my life, being transformed and my heart of stone being turned back into a heart of flesh. The thing with Al-Anon is that I can never finish the steps because as new people, places, and things enter my life, the steps have to be reapplied over and over. God is amazing and smart!!

God would use Al-Anon in several ways to promote my U-Turn back to Him, which by this point was getting closer. First, my Al-Anon group became the source of the Therapeutic Intervention I so critically needed. No Psycho-Therapist or Psychologist could have provided me with the quality of specialized therapy I found for free going through the 12 Steps and sitting in my Al-Anon circle. The depths of emotional healing I found by participating in my Al-Anon circle of women was unmatchable.

Secondly, my experiences in Al-Anon revealed the spiritual and physical framework God had chosen for me to use in the ministry He would give me later to serve women and girls. Al-Anon provided me with this model and some preparation for women's ministry.

One-on-one encounters with women, sitting in circles with women face to face, unmasking and sharing our true selves, candidly sharing our pain, and engaging in mentoring and supportive relationships have been the life-changing tools of my ministry to hurting and lost females for more than thirty years now. So, let's get back to the details of how this fantastic sequence of extraordinary events happened.

So, I found a meeting in the GlenCastle area. I joined the group. My sessions were held weekly on Thursday nights. In my Al-Anon group, the meetings were held with everyone seated facing each other in a circle. Our group was composed of all females. There was some diversity of color and age among the women in our group. Most of the women in my group shared their stories, and most of their stories included a painful past or present situation.

Many women in the group lived out their daily lives with family members who were addicts or alcoholics. Several of them had childhood experiences similar to mine that also involved an alcoholic parent or close relative.

In this Al-Anon group, I discovered that there were other women like me. That was a significant revelation. I always felt like I was the only little girl who had been sexually abused and was going through my kind of hell. In Al-Anon, I came to realize that keeping the lid bolted on my secret keg and making Dee (denial) my best friend had kept me mentally irrational and emotionally broken. Secrecy and denial had kept me living two different lives, feeling trapped, isolated, and thinking that I had to live my life, hiding my feelings and emotions.

For weeks in Al-Anon, I just listened. After the meetings, some women would stay around awhile to interact and get acquainted with the newcomers. That was how I learned who everyone's source of faith was. Eventually, I began listening to two of the Christian women in the group. We started talking regularly after the meetings.

Later on, they became what Al-Anon calls my Sponsors. I called them my mentors. They would call me between meetings to check on me and encourage me. Jesus used them to help begin to soften my heart of stone even more, and they kept pointing me to Him. They both encouraged me to read the Bible and suggested that the Book of John would be a good starting point.

Over time, I grew to trust these women, and I saw them as good examples. They had both endured a similar kind of painful childhood as mine, but unlike me, they had this inner peace and joy, and they were secure in who they were and self-confident. I had never come close to having any of those qualities. I began to feel that inner peace, joy, and self-confidence, but I had no idea how or where to find such qualities.

They were both married to husbands who were once substance abusers. I did not know then that a day would come when these two mentors would coach me through my real-life drama with a third husband who was a substance abuser. These two women would increase in value to me as the years rolled on. God placed them there. It was another set-up that would help me progress in my U-Turn back to Him.

Finally, I looked for and found a Bible. I began to try to read it now and then. I found it challenging to understand and gave up quickly. I eventually mentioned my difficulty to one of my mentors, who told me to start praying to understand what I was going to read before I started reading. She suggested again that I start my reading in the Book of John. I would start trying to read and stop, start again, then stop. Finally, I stopped and asked to understand it, but it was not really in the form of prayer. It was more like a spoken request. Jesus must have heard it as a prayer because my understanding did improve some.

The women who never revealed themselves as Christians in our group also had some traumatic stories to tell and were also making progress in their recovery process. I vividly remember one woman in our circle who told her heart-breaking story a couple of months after joining.

I could see and hear that she was making progress in her recovery from the horrific sexual abuse inflicted on her as a young girl. Her alcoholic father was her abuser, and after years of sexually abusing her, he began prostituting her out to the men who came into his back-woods Juke Joint. Her story made mine almost sound trivial. I would sit looking at her as she shared small portions of her gut-wrenching tale each week. I felt amazed as I witnessed the evidence of her survival and recovery, both emotionally and mentally.

I also heard testimonies from women who were victims of incest as young girls. I realized that despite what I had endured, it could have been worse. Al-Anon provided a place of awakening, gratitude, and hope for me and of seeing new possibilities.

God set me up to hear the women's stories in my Al-Anon circle because listening to their stories made me realize that I was not alone. I realized that many other little girls suffered too, many more greatly than I had.

Hearing their stories made me feel like I had finally found a place where I fit in, and no "people-pleasing" was necessary. I could safely exhale in my Al-Anon circle, which is what I slowly began to do.

My Al-Anon circle of women changed my life, and it was the God set-ups that were making the U-Turn happen. But wait until you hear what God does next using a bunch of notorious "bad girls"!!

I did not know this at that time, but God had already planted a passion for serving abused, hurting, and lost females inside my heart from my birth. That passion came alive due to my own experiences with being a little girl who was sexually molested. God had predetermined what my purpose would be and how He would use my life.

Before long, I would see that Al-Anon provided the framework I would begin to use in developing a ministry to the women and teenage girls at GlenCastle. Women seated in circles would become a permanent part of my ministry. God used Al-Anon to begin to turn my heart of stone into a fleshly heart that would soon receive Him back.

A "super-major" bolt was removed from my secret keg while in Al-Anon. As I exhaled, I realized that the women I had found in my Al-Anon circle were living proof to me that there could be joy, peace, and fulfillment for a girl after being sexually abused and rejected by the men in her life.

My Al-Anon mentors inspired me and encouraged me to begin reading my Bible, and I finally took a serious look at what the Book of John had to say. I was astounded by what I found out.

I was shocked to find out that there were some "bad girls" in the Bible and that Jesus spent time with some of them. I was mesmerized and drawn into the stories I read because I could see myself in each one of them. I also saw how each one of them came into Jesus's presence emotionally broken and weighted down, but each of them left emotionally restored and lifted. In John 4: 1-42, I read the whole story of this "bad girl" living in Samaria over and over. I immediately noticed some similarities between her and I.

In this biblical story, Jesus said He needed to go through Samaria. Jesus intentionally traveled out of His way to meet her at a well. She was a Samaritan woman. Jesus was a Jew. The Samaritan people were shunned by the Jewish people and seen as inferior. In addition to being a Samaritan, she had been married and divorced by five husbands and was at that time living with a man who was not her husband. Jesus deliberately went there to talk to this "bad girl" in person and help her understand who He was. He already knew she had hit her bottom (just like me) and that on the inside, she was looking for a new way to live (just like me), but He first confronted her with the truth of her moral and spiritual condition (just like He did me). She found her "new way" to live during her encounter with Jesus that day.

Jesus also knew that she would leave Him and go straight into the city and tell the men that she had met Him at the well and tell them what He had done for her.

Jesus chose to use this broken woman with a messed-up past to influence the men in Samaria and bring them to Him in a time when even an honorable woman would have almost no influence at all with men.

It would be even more impressive that it would be the men's knowledge of her reputation as a "bad girl" that would work in her favor. It was her story of how Jesus, a Jewish man, had shown her grace and acceptance that would compel them to see Jesus for themselves.

I began seeing Jesus like she was seeing Jesus. My heart was softening by reading her story. Because of this converted "bad girl," the shunned and ridiculed people of Samaria got to spend two entire days with Jesus in their town, and he saved many of their city!!

This "bad girl" came on the scene to perform the daily mundane task of filling her bucket with water and left the stage, leaving her bucket behind and going into the city as a missionary telling others what Jesus had done for her and leading them back to Him.

After those days spent with Jesus, I feel sure she felt new on the inside. Jesus changed the way she saw herself and how the people in the town of Samaria saw her. Jesus gave her a unique identity in Him. I began wanting that too.

When I was first reading her story, I didn't know I would one day be a commissioned Urban Missionary and that my "bad girl" conversion story would one day be used just like hers. I didn't know that like her, and I would one day come into His presence broken as I was, be healed, delivered, and restored, and go out as a missionary into the urban areas of Atlanta to tell my story and point others to Him. He knew what her story would do to me. He knew I was broken and hurting too. Jesus knew that I would feel what she felt because I was no different...I was just like her.

In John 8: 1-11, I read the story of another "bad girl" caught in the act of adultery by the Pharisees (religious leaders). They brought her in and placed her before Jesus in the temple. The Pharisees wanted to see how Jesus would respond to her situation, and they reminded

Jesus that Moses, in the law, commanded that she should be stoned to death. They asked Jesus, "What do you say?" After a while, Jesus said to them, "He that is without sin among you, let him first cast a stone at her. One by one, her accusers, being convicted by their conscience, turned and walked away.

He asked her if any man condemned her, she answered, "No man, Lord." Jesus said to her, "Neither do I condemn you. Go, and sin no more." She called Him Lord, indicating that Jesus held a position worthy of her worship and honor because He had ministered grace and mercy to her instead of condemnation.

I was like her too. As I read her story, I could feel the shame, guilt, and agony of my committed adultery. And I could feel the grace and mercy Jesus gave her because I needed it just as desperately as she did. I could feel what she felt because I was just like her. She would become my example of the unmerited and unconditional grace of Jesus Christ.

I found another "bad girl" who had been transformed by Jesus before her encounter with Him in Luke 7: 36-50. This "bad girl" was described as a woman who came in from the city, which meant she was believed to be a prostitute. Uninvited, she came into Simon's home, a Pharisee who had invited Jesus to come to dine with him.

She had brought an alabaster box of costly ointment. Jesus had lounged on the floor at the table with Simon when she came in and stood at His feet behind Him. She began weeping and began to wash His feet with her tears. She dried His feet with her hair, and she kissed His feet and anointed them with the ointment.

What she was doing for Jesus was her response to who Jesus was to her personally. He had already transformed her life. This was her way of showing her gratitude and love for Him. It was an act of pure worship. It was an intimate moment for her to freely and unashamedly show her devotion to Jesus. It didn't matter to her that she was not invited to come in or had an audience watching. All that mattered to her was Jesus. This prostitute's response to Jesus would later become my example of what my worship time with God should exactly be.

Contrary to what the other men at that table were thinking about her, Jesus, knowing her heart had been transformed, said to the men, "I say to you, her sins, which are many, are forgiven, for she loved much. But he who is forgiven little loves little. Then He said to her, "Your sins are forgiven."

This "bad girl" became the one I envied the most. I knew what hitting her bottom felt like. I was familiar with the bottom. But when Jesus said to her that her sins were forgiven, I knew that was what I wanted and what I needed to hear too.

I was like all of these " bad girls" and the numerous other "hurting women" Jesus had one-on-one encounters with like *the woman with an issue of blood for twelve years* (in Mark 5: 25-34), *the woman bowed over for eighteen years* (in Luke 13: 11-13) the *Canaanite woman and her demon-possessed daughter* (in Matthew 15: 22-28) and *Mary Magdalene who had evil spirits and infirmities* (in Luke 8: 2). He healed them all.

Additionally, there are others like Hannah, who was barren, Anna, who suddenly became a very young widow, and Esther was orphaned after tragically losing both parents. There are valuable lessons for every female living today in the lives of the biblical girls. The stories of the "bad girls" and "hurting women" in the Bible would become a permanent, handy, and beneficial tool throughout my ministry life and personal life.

I searched the Bible looking for them. Women who were forgiven, healed, restored, delivered, and set free by Jesus in intimate one-on-one encounters. I read all of their stories and knew it was time for my meeting. As I read, I could feel what He was doing for them. As I read, I felt what Jesus gave them and knew it was what I needed.

Jesus and His encounters with these women came alive to me and in me. Just as the Bible teaches that God's Word is supernatural and capable of doing remarkable things, it's true. I know this for myself.

I had a similar kind of feeling in my Al-Anon circle when I heard the stories told by the women there. I could feel what they had gone through or were going through as they spoke it. I didn't know that God had already deposited a special kind of compassion, caring, and love for women in my heart. His deposit would be withdrawn by me soon after, and a life-long ministry for *His Girls* would begin.

The simple truth for me was the same simple truth that had existed for all the "bad girls" of the Bible. In Isaiah 42: 3, Isaiah said it this way, *"A bruised reed He will not break, and a smoldering wick He will not snuff out."* He gave me beauty for my ashes. He gave me the oil of joy for my thirty-two-year long spirit of heaviness. Jesus overcame my evilness with His goodness. Why did He do that for me?

The *whole* truth is that what Jesus did for me was done long before I sang "Jesus Loves Me" at six-years-old and before the sexual abuse began. It was done before sitting in my Al-Anon circle and discovering the "bad girls" of the Bible.

It was done before the games with men began, before the divorces, before coming to Atlanta, and before becoming the undeserving recipient of the extravagant grace, mercy, forgiveness, kindness, blessings, patience, and lavish love Jesus bestowed on me despite my rejection and defiance.

It was done before He came seeking after me like a Shepard after *His* lost sheep. It was done before I was even born!

It was done in John 15:16 when Jesus said," *You did not choose me, but I choose you and appointed you so that you might go and bear fruit — fruit that will last.*

That was when Jesus choose me as *"His Girl,"* and nothing can or will ever change that!! Jesus did all these things for me because I belonged to Him—so do the "bad girls" and the "hurting girls," and so do you! If you are on this road trip with me right now (reading my story), you are chosen too, and you belong to Jesus whether you know it yet or not, and even if you intentionally turned and walked away from Him as I did.

Why do I say that? Because God set you up just like He set me up. Reading my story is a way God is using to win you over to Him. God, through His Son Jesus, has declared He has chosen you and appointed you to go and bear fruit that will remain. What is your response to God's plan to use your life for His purposes?

Finally, I could see clearly enough to repent, ask for forgiveness, and humble myself before Him gratefully. It was my turn to make my choice; I chose Jesus as my Savior. I gave my heart back to Him!! I made a U-turn!! *I admitted that I had sinned, and I asked for forgiveness of my sins. I told Him I believed Jesus was His son, and I asked Jesus to come into my heart and be my Savior.*

You can do the same thing right here and right now by saying what I said. You can give your heart and life to Jesus this very moment. If you do, if you ask Jesus to come into your heart, contact someone you know who is a committed follower of Jesus Christ and give them the good news!! Get a Bible and start reading the Book of John so you can start learning who Jesus is and how much He loves you. Find yourself a Bible-centered church to attend or view on-line. Seek out friends who are believers. I promise you that you will always be glad that you did.

If you gave your life to Jesus, I would welcome you to the Body of Christ, CONGRATULATIONS!!! You have made the most critical decision of your lifetime!!

For me, everything with Jesus happened in the activity of our ongoing one-on-one relationship. Over time, I would also embrace Him as.....my Lord, my healer, my restorer, and my deliverer who would set me free and give me a new life to live. I did not know or understand that Jesus had so much more for me. What God had done in my life was great, and He will do more because I am His project.

The completion of my transformation would take more time. I know you didn't think I was going to be some sort of an overnight sensation, did you? Good, because I wasn't even close. I still made some bad choices, practiced disobedience, and even got involved with another man in all the wrong ways. Jesus knew I was human and prone to sin. He always had a plan for me. When I choose to be *His Girl,* the project could proceed!!

I have written a description of what the next several years of my spiritual journey with Jesus as my Savior looked like in a later chapter. The story will give you an aerial view of how my spiritual journey to *His Girl entirely* happened.

I also have a visit with my father to tell you about, and I have another marriage coming up. Both of these life-changing events would become critical to my *becoming His Girl fully*. Right now, let's get back to GlenCastle and see what's up.

Chapter 8

GlenCastle
Pt. 3: The Launch

In this chapter, I will share the process God used to turn my pain into power!! First, you will see how God very gradually launches me into ministry, which climaxes with a scenario that took me face to face with my father.

Then you will see how God uses my bitter rain days to give other women hope. Just like the Samaritan woman Jesus met at the well, God would take what the enemy meant for evil in my life and use it for good! When I began to use my bitter rain days to help other women, my pain was turned into power.

My Al-Anon circle of women and my biblical "bad girls" had helped transform my thinking and open my heart back up to Jesus. What was once bitter rain to me would become the sweet rain of hope to other women just like me.

Please indulge me by allowing me to share a condensed overview of the ways God used me in ministry and share the names of some key people God used to make it all possible. Without the amazing people mentioned here, there would be no ministry to review. Here is how it happened.

I was back in the office at GlenCastle. It was about mid-summer of 1992 and maybe about fourteen months after starting Al-Anon and meeting those biblical "bad girls." I had completed my U-turn back to Jesus as my Savior about six months earlier.

My experiences in Al-Anon motivated me to install an additional step to my interviewing process with potential residents. I see this now as my first small assignment from God. My interviews were often with candidates that met our criteria and were likely to become a resident of GlenCastle. My interviewing process had always included the applicant telling me their story (life journey). Hearing their stories became my favorite part of the interview.

The new step I added on was me telling the applicant my story. I was amazed and delighted to see the positive responses to me candidly sharing my story. After sharing our stories, the person being interviewed and I seemed to have found some common ground and a shared connection with each other.

After the applicant became a GlenCastle resident, there was an unspoken rapport between us that made communications between us easier even when there were problems.

I also noticed how each time I shared my *bitter rain* story in an interview, another layer of shame, insecurity, and fear of what others might think was lifted off me. In other words, the more I shared my story, the freer I felt! With these benefits being discovered, my willingness to share my story increased.

A testimony or telling of our story is the *purest gift* we can give God. It is more refined than our praises, tithes, or even our worship because all these things can have unconscious human motives behind them. Our testimony is the purest gift because we gain nothing for ourselves. It is a pure gift to God because every time we give our testimony, we take a risk for God. We risk losing the admiration and praises of people by exposing our flaws, character defects, and weaknesses.

We risk offending or upsetting people who may feel convicted by our transparency or be reminded of unpleasant things in their own lives. By candidly and thoroughly telling our story, God alone gets the glory He deserves. You see, God can't get *all* the glory if we don't tell *all* the story. For me, a complete testimony includes what they did, what I did, and what God did. I believe that God is pleased with us and blesses us for sharing our stories because He is the hero in them, and others are pointed in His direction.

My next assignment was another one that I later identified as an "offspring" of Al-Anon and those biblical "bad girls." The project was to begin a women's Bible Study for the women at GlenCastle. When this desire manifested in my spirit and heart, I immediately knew what to do because Al-Anon had given me the framework, and the "bad girls" and the "hurting women" of the Bible had given me my topics. By this time, I had developed a desire to get to know all the women of the Bible and had begun studying them one by one. The Bible Study theme became "Women of the Bible." God had set me up perfectly for this assignment.

After I created an outline and a rough draft lesson plan, I sent out invitations to the building's women. I was excited and looking forward to having us make our circle of women at GlenCastle. I wanted us to share our stories and the goodness of God together. The response to my invitation was not great. Only a few women in the building engaged in participating consistently.

It was a smaller circle than I had hoped for, but God placed two exceptional women in the process. Their names are Michelle Murray and Angela Amica Ames. Michelle and Angela met at GlenCastle. Both were referred to us by a homeless task force. They were both single mothers having four children each, and both of them were former substance abusers having several years of clean time. Both Michelle and Angela attributed their deliverance from addictive substances and their families' restoration to their surrender to Jesus Christ and following His word.

They attended the Bible Study regularly and demonstrated their readiness and a sincere desire to grow spiritually. I shared everything I knew about Jesus and the women of the Bible and encouraged the women in our group to apply what they learned to their own lives, just as I was doing.

Our Bible study time also became a time to build a relationship with each other by intimately sharing our past experiences, day-to-day lives, and praying together for God's provisions. The Women's Bible Study I held at GlenCastle would become a life-long tradition of mine. I have established a neighborhood Women's Bible Study in every neighborhood I have lived in since then.

Today, Michelle, Angela, and I are still actively engaged and building on the twenty-five plus years we have shared following and serving God, as missionaries and as partners in ministry. They are my closest ministry associates and allies.

Today, both Michelle and Angela hold ministry degrees, and both are Ordained Ministers. Michelle serves as the Associate Pastor at her church and holds a Master's Degree in Pastoral Counseling. Both Michelle and Angela are authors with published books. You will hear more about them as we continue because they have played many active roles in my life and ministry. God set that up!!

With the new addition to the interview process in place and the Women's Bible Study humming along, I was expecting to cruise for a while. To me, these two new additions to my spiritual life were plenty. I was still running the office and leading the Spiritual Committee, which included Sunday morning service in our new chapel in the Blacksmith's Shop and Sunday School. We named our new chapel "The Chapel of Hope."

Yes, I was back in Sunday School and enjoying it as I did as a six-year-old. Rev. Love was doing a great job teaching Sunday School and providing the sermon for our Sunday services twice a month. A few residents formed a small choir. We also had a volunteer guest pastor who came once a month when Rev. Love could not be there. I thought my plate was full, and I was content, but God was thinking otherwise. He always has a plan.

God had given me a glimpse of this new assignment around the same time I worked through the Al-Anon step to reconcile with Suede, but this assignment was much more emotionally charged and risky. Compared to my first two spiritual assignments, this new assignment was a monster! So, I put it off and put it off, thinking it would eventually go away.

I did not know that this assignment would have to be completed before God would use me more in ministry. At that moment, I did not know there was anything more significant for me to do, but God was planning a launch out into the deeper waters of ministry for me. In other words, God was preparing me for public ministry.

My time for procrastinating had run out. I had been ignoring what I was hearing on the inside for over a year. I had been hearing inside that it was time for me to confront my father face to face. Now, you know why it took me so long to address this assignment.

The anger and bitterness I felt towards my father were gone. The desire for revenge was gone. God overtook my desires for evil with His desires for my good. There came a time where I had to spiritually let go of and rebuke the anger, bitterness, and revenge so there could be room for the extravagant grace, mercy, forgiveness, favor, provisions, and love that God was flooding into my new life!!

The profound blessings I was receiving from God had pushed out and left no room for anger. Jesus had overtaken my bitterness with His amazing grace and rich blessings. Along with my spiritual, moral, and emotional restoration, God had restored me economically with a good income, a great place to live, adequate medical insurance, and a newer, more reliable vehicle. Physically, Chiffon and I were well and healthy. God had even given me the ability to stop smoking. All I could feel was blessed and thankful!!

I kept hearing it is time to confront your father over and over on the inside. I believed that it had to be done. I thought it was God saying it and that it could be the next step in my restoration, emotional healing, and growth in Christ. It would be on my return trip home after seeing my father that God would give me a confirmation and an additional step to be taken once I arrived back at GlenCastle.

But, let's back up a little, so I can give you the inside scoop on how God set up the trip to see my father. Morganton was home for my father too, so there were times when he came home over the years. Eight of his thirteen siblings still lived in Morganton. I had seen him at several family gatherings over the years, and he always made a stop to see my mother while he was in Morganton, especially during the Christmas holidays. Before me telling my mother about the abuse (which was later on in my life), she had found her peace with his decision to leave us. She and my step-father allowed my father to visit us at their home and always treated him kindly.

Unaware of my father abusing me, Denim, Lace, and Satin could interact with him more freely. I was always civil towards him, not wanting to upset anyone or cause any concern. In other words, I kept my feelings under wraps as I had most often done. My insecurities and lack of self-esteem were still at work. His visits were usually brief, which worked out well for me.

When he left us, he moved to Connecticut, and many years later, he and a long-term female companion moved down to Lady Lake, Florida, and bought a retirement home. Lady Lake is a beautiful retirement community. The development they bought into was a golfing community with lots of extra amenities. Most people who lived there used their golf carts for transportation. It was as beautiful as any place you would see in a Florida retirement home real estate brochure.

I believed that God was saying that the time had come in my spiritual growth and healing process to confront my father face to face. As that little eight-year-old girl, I had no voice, no way of defending myself, no escape--only to endure it. But I had been rescued, healed, and given a voice by Jesus. It was time for me to find the courage to use it.

On the inside, I somehow knew not to expect any apologies or a request to be forgiven. Today, I know that was the Holy Spirit preparing me. I also knew on the inside that the purpose of the confrontation would be for me to finally speak up for myself and bring closure to my process of forgiving him so that I could move on. I also believed that God wanted him to be confronted with the truth for his own sake.

I couldn't just show up at his doorstep unannounced. So, I decided to take Chiffon along and invited Lace's daughter and Satin's youngest daughter promising them all a trip to Universal Studios in Orlando. They were very close in age, and my father barely knew these three beautiful grand-daughters.

When I spoke with him and his companion, they agreed that a visit from us would be nice. It would be a weekend trip driving down on Friday and returning on Monday. I planned the trip to Universal Studios for Saturday. I had a limited amount of time to get my assignment done.

We arrived safely. They came out with big smiles to welcome us, helped us unload the car and get settled in. It was about supper time, and they had prepared a meal for us. As we sat at the table eating, my father made a critical comment about the weight of one of my nieces, suggesting that she not overeat. I could not believe he was still so insensitive and thoughtless. His companion said nothing, and I let it go hoping my niece would ignore it until he made another insensitive comment about losing weight.

I could see the embarrassment on her face. I could tell her feelings were hurt. I mentioned that it was common for girls her age to go through weight changes. Later that evening, I found out that she was upset by what he said, and she wanted to go home. I reminded the three of them that we had planned the next day to go to Universal Studio and that we would be gone all day. I knew she did not want to miss that trip, and my father wasn't going with us. We made the trip to Universal Studios, but the damage was done, and she never became a fan of her grandfather.

We finished the meal and were sitting around watching TV. My father went out on his screened-in porch and began his drinking for the evening. His routine had not changed. I was tired, and he was drinking, so that was not a good time, and besides, we had just gotten there.

Saturday came, and I took the girls to Universal Studios, where I had as much fun as they did. When we arrived back at my father's house Saturday evening, he was out on the screened-in porch and already drinking. I kept hoping to find a time when he was not drinking, but I was running out of time.

After sleeping late Sunday morning, we had brunch together, and my father wanted us to go with him to visit some of his friends and neighbors and tour us around Lady Lake, which we did. We arrived back home in the evening, and he headed out to the screened-in porch. That evening was my final opportunity. He was drinking but had not had time to drink a lot. He was alone on his patio, so I prayed, and I gathered up my courage. I walked out there and sat down.

I began the conversation by saying I had something important I needed to share with him. I told him I remembered what he did to me as a little girl. I shared how I had struggled emotionally for years, and I talked about the damage it caused me. I also told him I had given my life to Jesus Christ a couple of years earlier and that He had healed and restored me from the abuse and was doing well.

He listened but never spoke. My Father's only response to everything I had said to him was, "He didn't know why he did those things." For me, this was an admission, but nothing more. God had prepared me well for that moment. God had let me know not to expect any expressions of regret or apologies coming from him. The meeting to confront him was for my benefit to get closure in my process. God had healed and restored me from what he had done to me. The anger and bitterness were gone. I felt free to move on with my life, and I was grateful to put our meeting behind me. I forgave him and let go for my own sake, so I did not have to hear his regrets or an apology.

On the trip back, I felt free, weightless, and so relieved. I would return to Atlanta changed by forgiving and letting go. On the drive back to Atlanta, in my mind, I was revisiting what God had done in Lady Lake when from inside me, I heard, "It's time to get the show on the road." God confirmed that it was time for me to launch out and begin to share my testimony publicly.

He let me know that step one would be to prepare my family. God said it was time for me to tell my mother, Lace, Satin, and Denim about the abuse and about confronting my father. I was finally ready to do that. I did, and I will share the encounter with my mother later.

God gave me time. I got a chance to show my father unconditional love and caring as his daughter, and I thank God for that, but the story does not end there. What God did next was amazing!!

God gave me a testimony that will encourage those whose spiritual and emotional growth has been cut off by holding on to unforgiveness. My story here is for anyone who feels they cannot forgive.

You can let it go. Give the offender to God. You can trust God with them. Forgive and let go of the anger, hostility, bitterness, and desire for revenge. Embrace the freedom, peace, and joy that letting go will bring you. Here is my story of the amazing thing God did.

About three years after I reconnected with my father, I got a call from his companion, the woman who had lived with him for almost twenty years. He was at home and had been sick in bed for weeks. His condition was deteriorating, not improving. He had lost a lot of weight and was getting weaker. The Ulcerative Colitis that had developed was not responding to the antibiotics he had been given.

She needed to go to visit some family members in another state. She asked if I would come back down to Lady Lake and take care of him for four days while she was gone. I said yes, as I had no real reason to say no, except that I would be out of my comfort zone. I had never spent any time alone with my father since my childhood.

On my second morning there, I woke up very early, around 5 am. From the inside, I heard, "Go in and pray with your father." I ignored what I heard and tried to go back to sleep. Again, I heard, "Go in and pray with your father." I started trying to rationalize my way out. My excuses were that it was too early; he was still asleep; he probably doesn't even believe in prayer. I tried to go back to sleep, but again and again, I heard it.

Finally, I sat up on the side of the bed. I was staying in the guest room. His room was just down the hall. Still looking for a way out, I peeked down the hallway at his room. His door was still wide open. I could see the chair I left by his bedside from the night before. I thought I would do it if he is awake; if not, I am off the hook. I tipped down the hall and stopped just outside his door. The lamp on his bedside table was off, but the light in the hallway was shining into his room. Hoping that he was asleep, I whispered, "Dad are you asleep?" My heart leaped when I heard him respond, "No."

I took an intense breath and stepped into his room. I did not turn on the lamp since the light was coming in from the hallway. I took another deep breath and eased down in the chair I had left by his bed the night before. I felt anxious but knew I had to do this. I asked him if I could pray for him, and to my surprise, he quickly answered yes. I extended both my hands, he placed one hand in mine, and I closed my eyes to pray.

I felt his hand in mine. I was startled by the hand I was feeling in mine. It was small and boney and frail—it felt little like a child's hand. My dad was a big man more than six feet tall with large hands,

155

but the hand I held felt much smaller than mine. I was thinking, "What is going on--whose hand is this? And from inside me, I heard, "This is the hand that molested you." Then I heard, "Now, who has the big hand? Who has the strong hand?" My hands felt bigger and stronger than my fathers' hand. At that moment, I knew God was showing me His justice on my behalf as that helpless little girl. I also knew that my father was not going to survive his illness.

I did manage to pray for my father that morning. I prayed for his healing and recovery and his comfort and peace. My whole heart's desire at that moment was that my Father would live and not die. I felt a deep sadness for him and the loss of the life he could have had.

At the same time, I felt very grateful that my sadness for my father was genuine and not mingled with any guilt or regret on my part. My response represented the evidence of God's healing and restoration in my own heart and life.

My father had told me a day or two earlier than he had given his life to Christ years ago. I hope that he did accept Jesus as Savior and that I will see him in heaven. My father died about six weeks later, never recovering from the Ulcerative Colitis.

After God helped me forgive and reconnect with my Father, He instructed me to ask my siblings to forgive and reconnect with him. Like me, they all had good reasons not to, but they also decided to reconnect after talking over everything.

My siblings are strong in their faith and unconditionally loving others just like our mother was. After we agreed, we began to try to connect with him in a more meaningful way. Our father had abused and neglected us all in some way. We had all suffered emotionally. On one of his trips to Morganton after my confrontation with him, the four of us sat down with him to talk. It was a planned meeting that we requested.

We each candidly shared our hearts regarding our past with him as our father, but we were respectful. He listened quietly as each of us spoke. He said very little. He gave no explanations and made no apologies but calmly said, "you all had a better life than I did." That spoke volumes to me and confirmed what I already believed. My father was an emotionally broken man that never got repaired.

The four of us took a trip down to Lady Lake to visit our Father for an entire week about two years before he died. He seemed to enjoy having the four of us with him, and He showed us off to all his friends and neighbors.

The four of us returned there together a few days before he passed in the hospital to spend time with him. He was in an unconscious state when we arrived and remained unconscious until he died. We sang hymns around his bed. We held his hands and told him repeatedly that we loved him.

We could easily do this not because of all the warm and fuzzy moments we spent with our Father, but because of who God was in our lives. The grace and mercy shown in our own lives was our motivation.

We also knew that it was what our mother would want us to do. Later in life, I discovered a positive side of my father's imprint, with some positive traits inherited from him, like my love of nature and the outdoors, my fondness for jazz music, and an appreciation of staying fit. He made sure my three siblings and I could swim and taught us how to pitch a tent and make a campfire. He was an intelligent and gifted man.

He achieved some successes before leaving our home town. I believe he became the first African American man in our county to earn the designation of Eagle Scout. He was a skilled swimmer and Springboard Diver. He was also probably the first African American man in our town to be hired by the city in a management position. He became the first director of the Recreation Center built for blacks in our town. He gave up that position when he chose to move to Connecticut.

My siblings and I chose to love him because he was our father. We were grateful that we had forgiven him and re-established our relationship with him, but none of us ever really knew him or bonded with him, and he never really got to know us. His companion and her children, friends, and neighbors in Florida and the four of us gathered for his Memorial Service, and all sorts of praises and accolades were spoken about him.

As I sat there listening, I smiled. All I could think of was the peace I was feeling. Forgiving my father and reconnecting with him had brought me that peace. I left Lady Lake with no regrets and fully recognizing how blessed I was. I believe that forgiving him was an greater blessing for me than for my father. God did that.

It is never too late to forgive. Forgive for your own sake. Receive the freedom and peace that forgiving will bring you. Vengeance belongs to God. Let God be the judge. He will uphold you. God is perfect in all His ways.

After arriving back at GlenCastle, I began working on a plan to meet with my siblings to tell them about the abuse. It worked out perfectly when we decided to have everyone come to Atlanta for that upcoming Thanksgiving holiday. I had an opportunity to sit down with Lace and Satin and share what had happened while they were here. Before they came, Denim and I had a chance to get together and talk. The result of all of this sharing was a tighter bond among the four of us and lots of support for me.

My mother was also here that Thanksgiving, but the time did not seem right for telling her. The whole holiday was centered around her, and she was so happy. So, I waited until later to visit with her at her home in Morganton.

So far, GlenCastle had been the home base for the extraordinary life-changing transformation that was occurring inside me and around me. There were more steps that God had planned for me to take while at GlenCastle.

I had added the telling of my story into the interview process. I had begun the women's Bible study. I had confronted my father. I had shared what happened with Denim, Lace, and Satin. I had made plans to see my mother to tell her what happened.

I had developed enough trust in God's process for my life that I found the courage to complete these steps. What came next would be more difficult for me. I would need more trust and courage than before to complete this step. The next step would be different from the others. The next step was to share my story at the FCS- Urban Ministries monthly staff luncheon. It would be my first step out into public ministry.

Each month, all the individual ministries under the FCS umbrella came together for a joint luncheon at the Stables (administrational office). FCS provided the meal, and each month a different associate, as we were called, would volunteer to share something inspirational with the group. The luncheons were well attended and would include Bob Lupton, the FCS President, and Nancy Flippen, the Charis Community Housing Director, who was also my boss.

Nancy was the person I met with the day I came in to apply for Interim Housing. She was the person who reviewed my resume, told me all about GlenCastle, and asked if I was interested in applying for the manager position. The years of support, encouragement, and kindness she extended to me while at GlenCastle will never be forgotten.

The room would be full of people who had encouraged, inspired, and believed in me since the day I drove up that hill. Many of them were present the morning of the GlenCastle Opening Celebration and had heard me read my infamous "opening prayer." Some persons present may have been on the interview committee the day I was interviewed.

So far, the step to confront my father had been the most challenging. I realized the other steps were more manageable for me because they were performed within my comfort zone. The people with whom I shared my story within the interviews fell within my comfort zone. I had close relationships with my family members. Even though my news was upsetting, I was still within my comfort zone with them. I would be a long way from my comfort zone, standing up, and sharing my story at the luncheon.

I became very anxious about it until I realized that my story wasn't about me. It was about Jesus! Jesus was the hero of my story! I was the victimized little girl who grew into an angry, bitter, and vengeful woman that Jesus had to come and rescue. But there was

161

more. The rescue alone wasn't enough for Jesus. He planned to bring me full-circle by reconnecting me to my abusive father through forgiveness and unconditional love so those hearing my story would know that He offers full restoration in their lives too.

I realized that my story no longer belonged to me. It belonged to Jesus and other females like me. That was how I became able to let go of my feelings of insecurity, lack of self-confidence, and constant thoughts of what people would think of me. I had to tell my story at that luncheon, and I did! It became the launching pad for my launch into public ministry.

The sharing of my story that day got a similar reaction from my fellow associates and the FCS and Charis leaders as it did from my applicants during the interviews.

Again, an unspoken rapport and a heightened ability to relate and to communicate with them just seemed to happen on its own. I received encouragement and guidance from Bob Lupton, who later opened many doors of opportunity for me as I continued to try to follow God's plans and purpose for my life. Bob's support, expertise, insights, kindness, and the time he spent mentoring me will always be appreciated and warmly remembered.

Back at GlenCastle, progress was also being made in the spiritual lives of Chiffon and I too. Chiffon had come home after spending some time with her best friend Velvet and asked if we could visit

Velvet's church. Velvet's parents had purchased a home through Charis Community Housing and belonged to a church nearby. We had been visiting churches, but we had not found the right one for us. Long story short, we visited Velvet's church, we joined in 1994 and spent twelve years there. It was Beulah Cathedral Church of Christ Holiness, USA, in Decatur, Ga. It was the perfect fit for both of us!

Beulah Cathedral became the source of many God sent blessings even until this day. My sisters in the church's women's ministry called United Christian Women's Ministry (UCWM) became a significant source of my spiritual growth and progress and constant support, encouragement, and help in my ministry efforts.

Over the years, while still at GlenCastle, God continued to move me towards public ministry by giving me more assignments at GlenCastle that would later transfer out into the urban community around me. My most passionate desire became to serve the hurting and lost women in the urban facilities of Metro Atlanta.

Before that ministry began, I discovered a more immediate need right in the building with the middle-school-aged boys who lived there. During the early nineties, Atlanta's housing projects and inner-city neighborhoods were being bombarded with gang activity that had sprung up, and it was growing at an alarming rate. The frequency of crimes involving boys in the 6th, 7th, and 8th grade age range was rising. Young boys were being sought out and recruited by two significant gangs around Atlanta.

Several boys were living at GlenCastle who could have been at risk, and many other boys this age living in nearby housing projects. I felt I had to do something to protect the boys in our apartment community, and I hoped to reach other boys living in the housing project. I expected both of these groups of boys would be served. God had provided me with the van to pick the boys up after school and provided a perfect location to meet right on our property. I established the Fit for the Kingdom After School Boy's Club in 1997 under the FCS umbrella.

God provided an adequate number of responsible Christian men and women who volunteered to serve as mentors and tutors. With the support and influence of Bob Lupton, and the commitment, abilities, and support of my amazing board, such as chairperson Lavon Chorba, enough funds were raised to provide ample supplies, equipment, and activities to keep the activities of the Kingdom Afterschool Boy's Club running for seven years. God provided the boy's club as a place of safety and nurture for young boys when it was truly needed.

In 1998, God opened up the way and allowed my passionate desire to serve hurting and lost women to become a reality. I hosted the first annual *Victorious Lady Seminar* (VLS) in the Chapel of Hope at GlenCastle for the women and teenage girls who lived in

GlenCastle. For twelve consecutive years, the VLS was provided to serve women from Metro Atlanta's substance abuse treatment facilities, homeless shelters, half-way houses, and battered women's shelters. The women from the facilities were always our *"guests of honor,"* the women from several churches and women from the surrounding community were also invited.

God provided everything needed through donated funds from committed Christians around Atlanta, through provisions from my church, and through one other "special anonymous resource" that gave faithfully every year to this event.

The primary focus or high point of the two-day event was to present *"real women with real stories"* as speakers who would share their stories of victoriously overcoming various adverse life-altering circumstances through their relationships with Jesus Christ.

Life-changing stories (testimonies) were told by real women that were invited to speak about their victorious survivals after being raped, addicted to Heroin, Crack, or alcohol, drug dealers, held at gunpoint, beaten and battered, incarcerated, victimized by incest and molestation, former prostitutes, homeless, choosing an abortion, subjection to witchcraft and other demonic and occult activities, having a mental illness and even murdering someone. There is nothing impossible for God and His Son Jesus!! There is nothing too hard for God!!

Each year, the event was planned and designed for women only. Men were always curious, but I never chose to invite men to attend due to protecting the privacy and comfort of all the women involved.

But in 2004, God flipped the script by making an addition. God began awakening me to two significant unaddressed needs of the women that I had been overlooking. One was their need to forgive the men who had harmed them (sound familiar?). The other was the need to realize that not all men were harmful. At that moment, I didn't know how much I needed to recognize that men who genuinely care for women do exist. But, God knew how much I needed it, and He made sure that it happened for all of us.

So, God said, I needed to provide an opportunity for the women to consider forgiving the men who had harmed them. And to give them a face to face encounter with some men who were genuinely caring and compassionate. I thought, "I need some "Brothers Who Care" (BWC). That was it!

When I asked God how, the name of a beloved pastor friend of mine, Elder Ronald Moore, popped into my mind. Pastor Ron, as I affectionately called him, often told his story of how God had granted him his greatest desire. After delivering Pastor Ron from years of drug addiction, God restored his marriage to the love of his life and reunited their family.

He was the pastor of Welcome All Church of Christ Holiness, USA, in College Park, Ga. I gave him a call and told him about the two new revelations God had given me for the women. I shared the vision God had given me of the men's roles and told him I needed some *"Brothers' Who Care"* (BWC) for the VLS coming up later that year. Pastor Ron took it from there.

I connected Pastor Ron with Rev. Tyrone E. Barnette, who had graciously invited me to use his church (Peace Baptist Church in Decatur, Ga.) for the VLS event after it had outgrown the facilities Beulah Cathedral Church two years earlier. Pastor Barnette initially made this offer based only on the purpose and objective of the women's event. When we met, he shared with me that he had been carrying a heart's desire to serve the women in the facilities for a long time without any viable opportunity to do so. After talking, we both knew we were the beneficiaries of another one of God's divine setups.

Pastor Ron and Pastor Barnette's hearts were a perfect match. They quickly bonded and began to recruit a group of men they believed were approved by God to minister to hurting women. Together, the two of them hand-picked about thirty men, both black and white, who would serve as the "Brothers Who Care" over the remaining years of the event.

Pastor Ron immediately recruited pastor George Terrell. He became the third piece of the "triangle of pastors" who led the effort to usher hundreds of women into God's presence where they could be saved, forgiven, delivered, restored, and set free during the Victorious Lady Seminars.

Stanton Lanier, an internationally known pianist living in the Atlanta area, also became a unique and faithful *Brother Who Care's* and a favorite at the event. His piano performances at many of the VLS events brought the women hours of comfort and peace.

Today, Stanton continues to communicate with me periodically and always mentions how delighted he would be to share his gift again with the women I serve.

Of all the unique ways God blessed hurting and lost women during the years of this event, the Brothers Who Care altar ministry became an irreplaceable favorite of our guests.

The "Brothers Who Care" altar ministry and the "real stories by real women" components became an unbeatable combination for making a meaningful, positive and permanent impact on the women who were served by attending the   Victorious Lady Seminars.

The "Brothers Who Care" altar ministry became another piece in my collection of over the top priceless sweet rain events. It was so impactful that I want to try to express what I saw, felt, and heard as I sat amongst the women in the sanctuary each year. Try to imagine it with me. Maybe God will do something supernaturally for you as I share how the BWC ministry made me feel.

The BWC began serving the women the moment they arrived for the Friday evening service. Each year, the BWC would prepare the Friday evening meal. The favorite menu was grilled hot dogs and hamburgers with all the fixings, including dessert.

Some of the men served as van drivers who picked up some of the women from the facilities. When the vans pulled into the parking area, other men would go out to meet the ladies, help them off the vans and escort them directly into our gaily decorated fellowship hall for a fellowship meal served by the BWC before the evening service.

This not only made our guest feel good; it made all the women volunteering feel good too. One year, Stanton Lanier did a candlelight piano concert while the women enjoyed their meal by candlelight. I think the BWC did chicken that night...the women loved it!!

Each year, I had double-duty during the BWC altar ministry. I was there seated in the pews as a needy recipient of what God would do through the BWC. I was also on the VLS hospitality team assigned to provide hugs, comfort, and the Kleenex that were always needed during the BWC altar ministry.

Once the BWC men began to minister, it became difficult to tell who was on the hospitality team and who was a guest because all of us would be weeping.

Of course, there is nothing like being there in person, but here is my written description of what the BWC altar ministry experience portrays.

After eating lunch on Saturday, the women were all seated in the sanctuary listening to worship music. Some years as many as 200 women were attending.

First, the men dressed in all black would appear. Several men, usually about ten (all pastors or ordained ministers), would enter the sanctuary from the rear and walk single file down the aisle and form a line across the front at the altar.

Another single file line of about fourteen men dressed in black would enter from the rear and station themselves along the sanctuary's left wall. Simultaneously, another single-file line of fourteen men dressed in black would enter from the back and station themselves along the sanctuary's right wall. These men in black were men of faith who had been recruited by the three lead pastors.

The men had volunteered to stand on the walls surrounding us to represent a protection line, caring, and support for the women. They were husbands, dads, brothers, fathers, grandfathers, uncles, or sons chosen by the three lead pastors. All the men involved in BWC were from either Peace Baptist Church, Beulah Cathedral Church, or Johnson Ferry Baptist Church in Marietta, Ga.

The men were almost surrounding us in the sanctuary. I cannot fully describe it, but I could feel something shift in the atmosphere every year when the men entered and took their place. The presence of God filled the sanctuary. These men were there on an assignment from God to minister support to us as women. Their presence mingled with the supernatural presence of God in the sanctuary, and tears of the women would begin to flow.

Before all the men were through taking their places, sobs and weeping would begin and be heard throughout the sanctuary. The lament was an uncontrollable response to seeing so many men unified for our benefit in that environment. The women from the facilities were crying, the women from the churches were crying, all of us were crying. I always tried to dry my tears enough to move out to comfort other women. Usually, we all just ended up crying together.

The men on the walls stood on the walls throughout the service. Without a word spoken from them, the fact that they were there communicated their message loud and clear. It was a message of protection, caring, and affirmation of our value.

Pastor Ron, Pastor Barnette, and Pastor George usually spent the morning before the service preparing all the men. Each of the pastors and ministers up front had been assigned a different male role in a woman's life that could have caused her harm. Each man usually wore a name tag identifying his role. There would be men upfront who would portray a husband, father, boyfriend, pastor, son, "baby-daddy," drug dealer, brother, youth pastor, pimp, grandfather, etc.

One by one, each man would identify himself as the man he was portraying and apologize to the women in the audience and tell us how sorry he was as authentically as possible. After apologizing, each man would ask the women in the audience to please forgive him for the pain and damage they had caused them. Weeping and sobbing increased as the men spoke.

After all of the men had spoken, the women in the audience were invited to come up to the altar and form a single file line in front of the man playing the role of their real-life offender if they would like a prayer. The woman could choose to receive blessing from more than one man if she needed to do that. Each man was prepared to pray individually for each woman in his line. Each pastor or minister took time to listen, pray, and minister to each woman individually in his line.

The whole scenario was so hearted touching that some of the pastors and ministers would begin weeping, especially when they saw the number of women coming down the isles to join in the prayer lines. I saw tears in men's eyes and the looks on their faces as they saw the numbers of women who had been damaged by men in their lives. The pews were almost emptied each year.

My three lead pastors were all "cry-babies" every year at this event. That's why God chose them. They authentically cared deeply about hurting women. For a victimized woman, the sight of tears coming from a man's eyes because of his compassion for her probably made an unforgettable impact. It always did for me.

After the BWC altar ministry, a call to salvation was made, and the service closed in prayer. Afterward, our guest was invited downstairs to the church's basement for a "Pampering Party," including foot baths, nail painting, shoulder massages, perfume samples, a clothes and shoe pantry, and gift bags as they departed.

Today, Pastor Ron and Pastor George are celebrating together in heaven. Pastor Barnette is still going strong, and the Brothers Who Care concept still lives on. After Pastor Ron passed, Pastor Barnette wanted to do something to honor Pastor Ron. In 2016, we put our heads together and planned a one-day event for the Brother's Who Care to serve the women of Peace Baptist Church and women in the surrounding community in honor of Pastor Ron. Pastor Ron's family were our guests of honor.

Later, Pastor Barnette and I shared how grateful we were that God had allowed us to provide a fitting celebration in honor of Pastor Ron's life and legacy.

In 2006, with the blessings of Bishop Smith at Beulah Cathedral, I transferred to Peace Baptist Church with Pastor Barnette, and he formally licensed me as a missionary in 2007 during a Sunday morning service.

In 2009, after twelve consecutive years, I retired the Victorious Lady Seminar event. But God had placed a burden for serving teenage girls in the heart of a young woman named Renay Allen, who was also a Beulah Cathedral Church member. I knew her well and was elated when she called me to let me know the assignment God had given her.

She wanted to transform the Victorious Lady Seminar into the Victorious Young Lady Seminar. Because of Missionary Renay Allen's passion, faithfulness, and obedience, teenage girls all around Metro Atlanta were invited to enjoy and benefit from the Victorious Young Lady Seminar for ten more consecutive years.

A team of missionaries, including Michelle and Angela (from the first GlenCastle women's Bible study) and many other women who had become missionaries through the academy, joined forces with the women in the United Christian Women's Ministry at Beulah Cathedral Church. Together, we provided support and assistance to Missionary Allen throughout the ten years she coordinated and directed the Victorious Young Lady Seminar.

In January of 1999, I was commissioned as a missionary by Elder Clifton Montgomery at Beulah Cathedral COCHUSA. At that same time, Elder Montgomery also commissioned me to become the

Community Chaplain at GlenCastle. Elder Montgomery would become a source of encouragement, sound guidance, accountability, and he always challenged me toward greater and bolder works for the Kingdom of God. When I look back now, I see that he was what I needed, when I needed it. I am still inspired today by his example of courage, confidence, and accomplishments that have come from always staying grounded in the Word of God.

Once again, Bob Lupton helped me by opening up an opportunity to transfer from my manager position at GlenCastle to becoming the Community Chaplain. The chaplain position was a part-time position, which freed me up to finally begin going into some of the women's facilities in Metro Atlanta.

I was very grateful and so excited. With an introduction and recommendation from Lavon Chorba to the director, I began my Urban Missionary entry into The Atlanta Day Shelter for Women and Children.

With the new work arrangement as Community Chaplain at GlenCastle, I was able to keep the Fit for the Kingdom Boy's Club going several more years. I closed the boy's club in 2004.

God opened the doors for me to serve the women at The Atlanta Day Shelter for Women and Children first. Then opportunities over the years were opened to help the women at Carp of Georgia, St. Jude's, View Point, My Sister's House, House of Hope, and Dekalb

County Jail (as a Volunteer Chaplain). My assignment at each facility was to provide a weekly Bible Study/Support Group. I usually did two Bible Studies per week.

In 2004, God opened a door for me to begin doing street ministry to women on the streets in the East Atlanta community and the Grady Hospital and Auburn Avenue areas near downtown Atlanta. I later added on ministering to homeless women in the parks in the same vicinity.

My passion for street ministry began through a phone call from an associate of mine from FCS. Her name was Linda Langstraat. Linda was the director of a ministry at FCS called Adopt-a-Grandparent. She was calling because of a request she had received from a group of senior-aged women served by Adopt-a-Grandparent. Adopt-a-Grandparent recruited teens, college-age, and adult volunteers and paired them with senior-aged persons who wanted to develop an ongoing relationship and receive home visits from someone who enjoyed relating to seniors.

The group of senior-aged women who contacted her had formed a weekly Bible Study group in one of their homes in the East Atlanta neighborhood. Linda reported that the group had faithfully been meeting for several years. Linda sometimes attended their Bible Study and knew of their heartfelt concern for their neighborhood, which was deteriorating due to the negative effects of poverty, crack cocaine sales, prostitution, and various crimes.

The women in the group decided to call Linda to see if she knew someone who might come to their neighborhood and minister to the numerous prostitutes walking the street of their neighborhood. Linda described these senior women as having heavy hearts due to watching these young women and not doing anything to help them. I attended one of their Bible Study gatherings to personally hear what was on their hearts. When I left there, I was convinced that it was another God ordered assignment for me.

I ask God how? I knew it would have to be ministry done on the street wherever I would encounter them, but I did not think walking through their neighborhood alone would be a good idea, even in the daytime. As I drove around the area, I was thinking about God? I drove past a busy little section where there were a few open small businesses.

I noticed a fair amount of foot traffic in this area when I saw the Family Store operated by one of the ministries under the FCS umbrella. I felt a setup coming on. When I saw that the Family Store was located right at the corner of Jonesboro Road and Confederate Avenue, I knew it was the right spot. I also saw how I could do it. God had worked it all out.

Long story short, I sat up a card table with two chairs right on the sidewalk in front of the Family Store. I made a large styrofoam sign printed with big black letters saying "Prayer Station," and I let people passing by know I was open. Yes, the girls prostituting frequently walked this street, and I got to meet, pray for, and get to know many of them along with a variety of homeless and discouraged people.

The "Prayer Station" ministry took a level of boldness that I severely lacked at that point, but I knew I was in the right place at the right time, so I persevered. As I look back on 2004 and beginning street ministry, I see the Prayer Station as another experience that God set up that would benefit my growth as it helped those I was assigned to serve. The "Prayer Station" ministry caught on and spread. It is still being used today by our circle of missionaries at both outdoor and indoor events. Where there are people, there will always be someone who needs prayer.

In 2017, God opened up an opportunity to use everything I had learned about street ministry during a two-year assignment in the Fulton Industrial Boulevard area located East of Atlanta near Six Flags Over Georgia. Fulton Industrial Boulevard had been known for years as the most notorious and crime-infested area in Atlanta. This area's notoriety was known nationwide because of the shocking amounts of crime, including illegal drug sales, violence, prostitution, strip clubs, and sex trafficking involving young girls.

Missionary Tonya Cook of Grace Walkers Ministry was already serving people in that hotel area and requested our help. We began by setting up a Prayer Station under a large tree on the corner of a street where three hotels were positioned close to each other.

A few weeks later, we discovered a church having Sunday morning services in the ballroom of the hotel located just across the street from our Prayer Station.

Pastor Lakisha Thomas had secured the ballroom and established services a couple of months before we got there. Pastor Lakisha provided various resources for her congregation, including a home-cooked meal every Sunday after service. The church congregation was made up of women with children who lived in the hotels on the block, a few people from the neighborhood, homeless men, and anyone who would come in off the streets to get the meals we offered. I served along-side Pastor Lakisha and her associate, Ms. Ruth, for two years.

God had given me a wide range of diverse experiences as an Urban Missionary and experience as a chaplain to be well equipped for my upcoming assignments.

Our twelve year stop at GlenCastle has come to an end. In the early summer of 2003, I was sensing that my time at GlenCastle was winding down. Inside I felt a change was on the way.

By late July, I heard what the change would be. God was calling me away from GlenCastle to begin what He called a "missionary academy" to prepare and equip women to become missionaries. I felt I was directed to resign from the Chaplaincy position.

This wasn't an easy thing for me to hear for many reasons. First of all, I had developed an emotional attachment to GlenCastle and FCS during the twelve years I had been there. My life had been transformed during those years. I saw FCS Urban Ministries and Charis Community Housing as my "spiritual incubator" where I had been fed and nurtured in a perfect environment of acceptance, opportunity, support, guidance, and encouragement. I knew it was time to step out of the safety of the incubator and follow God into a new season that would require a greater level of trust in Him alone.

However, there was that rational side of me that was making some good points. Points like I needed the income from the part-time Chaplaincy position to make ends meet. I would lose the small amount of medical insurance coverage available for Chiffon and I through Charis.

I also knew that the charitable contributions to my ministry could likely decrease if I left FCS. Leaving GlenCastle and FCS would be a complicated and risky move. I was hearing God directing me to resign to begin full-time ministry establishing a missionary academy, but that was all I was hearing. God gave me no instructions on how or where this would happen.

I struggled with what I heard and with God not giving me any answers. No other responses were provided. It would be a massive step out into a vast unknown for me. After days spent thinking and going over all of the what-ifs, the direction to leave was still right there.

On my birthday, September 4, 2003, I submitted my letter of resignation and began the process of leaving my beloved GlenCastle and FCS Urban Ministries (known today as Focused Community Strategies.) I was given a fantastic departure celebration that was running over with well wishes, encouragement, and promises of prayers from all my associates at FCS and all my residents at GlenCastle.

For several more years GlenCastle continued to provide affordable apartment homes for low-income individuals and small families. Today, GlenCastle and the adjacent property has new owners and is being converted into what is described as a complex offering *"creative office spaces."* As the centerpiece of this modern-day office complex, GlenCastle still looks beautiful and can continue to be a place of hope where entrepreneurs dreams may come true.

As I departed, the only place I could think to turn was to my church, Beulah Cathedral Church. After I turned in my resignation, I called the church to let my pastor know. Bishop Victor Paul Smith was serving as the interim pastor at that time. I knew Bishop Smith well. He was one of the first Brothers Who Care to be recruited by Pastor Ron. Bishop Smith had achieved a high level of respect, influence, and regard within the Church of Christ Holiness USA framework. Yet, he had the perfect temperament and personality for being a warm, caring, and supportive pastor. He was also an excellent example of a husband and father.

I made an appointment to go in to see him, not knowing what the outcome might be. I explained what God had said and told him that God had not given me any other directions or provisions. Thankfully, FCS had given me the approval to keep my mailing list of donors and the freedom to utilize the plan to continue to generate as much support as possible. I shared this blessing with Bishop Smith.

He asked me what I needed. I explained that I needed classroom space for the Fit for the Kingdom Boys Club and office space to begin my new assignment. I explained that if I were successful in establishing the Urban Missionary Academy, I would need a classroom to hold classes.

As soon as I finished my list of needs, Bishop Smith told me to go down the hall from his office and pick out the rooms I wanted to use. He said I could begin as soon as I needed. In a matter of minutes, God had provided everything I needed for office and classroom space through my pastor. It felt as if Bishop Smith already knew what I needed and was just waiting for me to get there and ask. I was so grateful and so relieved.

I went into that meeting with Bishop Smith, not knowing how any of this would work out, and when I came out less than an hour later, I had everything I needed to begin to fulfill my new assignment. God set me up again. I was full of hope and very excited.

When I began writing the curriculum for the women coming to the academy, many of the curriculum lessons were centered around developing a one-on-one intimate relationship with Jesus Christ. Several of them focused on those biblical "bad girls" and "hurting women. I know you are not surprised to hear that.

As soon as I started making some headway on creating the curriculum, God interrupted me to let me know I would enroll in graduate school. I know, that's what I said too. How?

God did it! In April of 2006, I graduated from Southwestern Christian University in Oklahoma City, Oklahoma, with a Masters in Ministry Degree in Christian Leadership.

A final requirement to graduate is called a Graduate Project similar in difficulty and volume to a thesis in a liberal arts university. Guess what?

The creation of the missionary academy and the curriculum became my Graduate Project. Who else but God could set up this kind of situation where completing my assignment from *Him* to create a missionary academy would turn out to be a perfect Graduate Project. What a set up that was!!!

I originally named the academy Esther's Urban Missionary Academy but changed the name to The Diamond Academy in 2015 to honor the academy graduates who God gave the name "Diamonds." The academy came to life on May 20, 2005, when the doors were opened to our first students: Lillie Estes, Dawn Montgomery, and Beverly Owens. This class graduated during a formal commencement ceremony on February 18, 2006. The academy was first established at Beulah Cathedral COCHUSA and was later transferred to Peace Baptist Church for the remaining years. The academy closed in June 2018 with a total of forty-two graduates. Thirty-two of them were formally commissioned as missionaries.

Among this group were Michelle Murray, Angela Ames, Renay Allen, and Linda Holland, who have never failed to stay connected and assist me in my ministry endeavors. Many of the academy's missionaries became instrumental in the Victorious Lady and the Victorious Young Lady Seminars while maintaining their own ministry assignments.

Some of them serve in key leadership positions in their churches. Others have established outreach ministries and street ministries in their communities and neighborhoods. Still, others are routinely ministering to people in their workplace, in their own homes, and in their extended family. Recently some have established online and telephone ministries.

Today, providing prayer support for each other, participating on our GroupMe page, teaming up to help each other with our ministry events, and attending fellowship events are the shared activities that keep us connected as Diamonds and missionaries.

After the final Diamond Class graduated in 2018 and my two-year service out on Fulton Industrial Boulevard with Pastor Lakisha Thomas ended, I began hearing that small voice inside saying I would be leaving Peace Baptist Church. This is when the reality that I was a missionary hit home. I realized that changes in location and changes in assignments were part of the calling as a missionary.

During the last few months at Peace Baptist, I began tying up any remaining loose ends in the ministry at Peace Baptist Church. I notified Pastor Barnette, who responded that God had already told him I would be leaving a couple of years before contacting him.

Pastor Barnette wrote me a beautiful letter of reference. I had an opportunity to express the tremendous impact he had made on me as my pastor and teacher and the life-changing experiences of serving women alongside him. I exited from Peace Baptist Church in July 2019.

This time, God wasn't saying anything about another church, but God had given me another assignment that had the potential of leading me back out into the urban community. I had been working on the administrational portion of an assignment God had given me early in 2018.

The assignment was to establish the Atlanta Urban Missionaries Association, Inc. (AUMA), a 501 c3 non-profit organization. I completed the administrational portion of establishing AUMA in August of 2018. AUMA became a legal entity, but God had not given me any enduring or productive means of utilizing AUMA. The only thing I knew for sure was that AUMA would be a platform to promote, inspire, encourage, support, and unify missionaries and continue to serve to hurting and lost women.

My dream since 2003 to serve women of every color and age had developed into a passion that I wanted to pursue, but nothing was happening, and I felt no sense of immediacy. God wasn't signaling anything except to wait. It was as if AUMA was a blank canvas, and I was the artist waiting to be inspired by God to paint.

Then, one day in early June of 2019, I got a phone call from Missionary Michelle Murray informing me that the United Way of Greater Atlanta offered community groups or organizations some free training that could lead to receiving a small grant. We were required to have at least five people on our team to enroll in the training class. That was the spark God used to set things in motion.

Michelle, Angela, Renay, another missionary named Bernadette Futrell, and I formed the AUMA Team and were accepted into their Community Building Institute. After completion, we received a small grant, which enabled us to begin serving the women and girls in transitional housing facilities and residential facilities in DeKalb

County, Ga. We got off to a good start and had established some regularly scheduled weekly and monthly visits to a homeless shelter for families until Covid 19 arrived and abruptly ended our efforts.

The blank AUMA canvas now has at least a few paint strokes. Being sidelined during the epidemic has given me plenty of uninterrupted time. One of the ways I have used this time is to finish this book. With God, there is good to be found in everything.

Three and a half months after exiting Peace Baptist, I still was not hearing anything from God about joining a new church, but I knew God had a plan.

Late in October, the setup happened through Missionary Linda Holland, who had volunteered as my administrative assistant for several years. She called to tell me about this church she had recently visited. She was excited to tell me that I should see this church because she thought it would be perfect for me. Listening to her description of the pastors, the service, and the congregation, it did sound like I should at least take a look.

When I hung up the phone, I immediately heard on the inside, "Go visit," and I did. I went the following Sunday morning, joined the Intercessory Prayer small group the next Wednesday, enrolled for new members classes, and made plans to join the church. I have been a member for over a year now. My impressive new church is Mountain West Church in Tucker, Ga. Pastor Michael and Elaine

Shreve serve in the lead position, and they are a fantastic ministry duo. Mountain West is the perfect church for me in this season of my life. Everything about it fits me.

GOD DID ALL OF THIS!!! HE PREDESTINED AND EXECUTED EVERYTHING!! What will He do next? I don't know yet, but I AM ALL IN!!!

However, the very most important things God has done for me were done behind the scenes, not out front while doing ministry, but behind the scenes in my one-on-one interactions with Him. That was where God (through the Holy Spirit) provided the perfect environment to bolster my spiritual growth and provide the emotional healing to become more effective in ministering to other women. My third marriage was the environment God choose to use for that purpose. I will share that experience with you in the next chapter. So, read on, and I will meet you there.

Chapter 9

I Do!

In this chapter, I will take you behind the scenes and show you the real-life process that God used to renew my mind, mold and reshape my character, break a generational curse and give me a new identity.

Like me, some people may not understand that there are two different decisions to be made when giving your life to Jesus Christ. I had done the easy part, which was admitting my sin, asking to be forgiven, and receiving *Him* as Savior. Jesus had done all the work on the cross. He had surrendered, sacrificed, and suffered for me to receive salvation freely.

I didn't understand that Lordship was as critical as salvation if I wanted the full benefits of a relationship with Jesus Christ. Surrendering to His Lordship required a lot of spiritual work on my part. Lordship needed me to offer my will and *trust His will* for me.

Do you remember that substantial unyielding problem I had trusting men? The time came to deal with it. It began with learning to trust Jesus.

Surrendering was a monster size ordeal for me. Here is that aerial overview I promised you. Looking back on the entire process, it felt like giving up my right to drive my own car. Here is how I would describe it.

When I met Jesus, I was driving down the road of life alone, and I had many wrecks.

After meeting Jesus and asking Him to be my Savior, I allowed Him to join me, and I made Him my front seat passenger. I continued driving my car down the road of life with Jesus as my passenger. I was still deciding all the stops and turns, but I was enjoying not being alone anymore. I still had a lot of wrecks.

A little farther down the road, I was still doing all the driving but allowed Jesus a little input in the stops and turns. I still had several wrecks but noticed I had none when I followed Jesus' directions.

A little farther down the road, I was still doing all the driving but decided to allow Jesus more input into my stops and turns. I had no wrecks when following Jesus' directions, but my chosen stops and turns were still ending up in impacts.

A little farther down the road, I got tired of having wrecks, so I ask Jesus to drive. I got in the front passenger seat. Sometimes I didn't like the direction He took and complained, but I noticed there were no wrecks.

A little farther down the road, Jesus was still driving, and there had been no wrecks at all. I decided to get in the back seat, get comfortable, and relax. The side views out the windows were scenic and relaxing. I felt good. I found out that I could trust Jesus to drive. I decided to stay in the back seat.

Accepting Jesus as Lord means He does all the driving. Total surrender to Him was necessary if I wanted to live a wreck-free life, but it took me a long time to move from under the wheel to the back seat. I finally got there, and God used my third marriage to do it.

It all began with another God setup, like everything else in my life. I first found out about Godly designs in the Bible (see Psalm 139:16). I found out that God had already written out all the days planned for me in *His book* before I was born. Based on what the Bible says, God has pre-planned every one of my days until my final one here on earth, and then I get to spend eternity with Him in heaven!

God used the marriage setup to mature and strengthen me spiritually, teach me patience, teach me how to trust and rely on Him, and find the good in adverse situations. It began with me pleading with God to take the wheel after I had the biggest wreck ever. I didn't know I was in for a nineteen-year journey that would include lots more bitter rain and just enough sweet rain.

This process began in real-time in 1993, while I was still just a "babe in Christ." It had been about a year and a half since I asked Jesus to be my Savior.

My third husband and I met at GlenCastle, of course. A substance abuse treatment facility operated by Oakhurst Baptist Church in Decatur, GA had referred him. At least one year of sobriety was required to apply for housing at GlenCastle. He had recently celebrated one year of sobriety. Oakhurst Baptist Church employed him as the church janitor. The director of the men's recovery program and the church pastor had written letters of reference. He appeared to be a good candidate for residency at GlenCastle.

In the interview, I found out that he had a long history of heroin addiction, including many "clean times" that ended with "relapses." I shared my story with him and the outcome, which was my decision to accept Jesus Christ as my Savior. For me, it was a routine interview that went well. I selected him as a resident, notified him, and he moved in.

Weeks later, I left my apartment and headed down the hallway towards the stairs when he stepped out of his apartment into the hallway. I didn't realize I had given him a unit on my side of the building. I remember him saying hello and us chatting for a moment.

Sometime later, we ran into each other again in the hallway. This time, I could tell that he was interested in me. We talked for a few minutes. Based on his conversation, he appeared to be intelligent and respectful and was well dressed. He had a very easy-going and appealing personality.

After we chatted for a few minutes, he asked me if I liked going to the park. Grant Park was walking distance from GlenCastle. I responded that I liked the outdoors and enjoyed going to the park. He said, "Maybe we could go over there sometime," and then he asked about going later that week. I thought a moment and said, "okay."

I have chosen the name Leather for him because he loved leather jackets and coats and leather furniture, but only if it was genuine Leather. His taste leaned towards the finer things in life, including clothing, shoes, jewelry, houses and furnishings, cars, food, and lifestyle. Even while working as a janitor and living in a recovery center, his appearance and clothing were always impeccable. He was six feet two inches tall, slender, as dark as an Oreo cookie and his smile resembled the center filling of the Oreo.

All we did on the park outing was talk, talk, talk. He told me about his only child, a son who was the same age as Chiffon. He told me about his mother, whom he said he adored, and his favorite aunts and his male cousins and his brother. It sounded like he loved his family as much as I loved mine. I told him all about my mother,

Denim, Lace, and Satin and how I loved going home to North Carolina.

We talked about our past and our hopes for the future. I shared my passion for serving the hurting and lost women and the church I had recently joined. He shared his desire to help troubled boys and his desire to use his story to steer them away from using drugs. He told me that he had recently given his life to Jesus Christ and joined his mother's church. He was scheduled to be baptized soon. He invited me to come to his baptism service at his church.

Several days later, I attended his baptism service and convinced myself that Jesus Christ was transforming his life like me. I met his mother that day, and a favorite aunt, and they were both delightful.

I never stopped to ask God what he thought about Leather. I was still doing the driving, but I had left my game playing with men behind. I still wasn't trustful of men, but I felt I was in a new place and got a fresh start.

Leather came on the scene before the effects of my budding relationship with Jesus had taken hold and soaked in. I had limited exposure to God's Word and was far from understanding and applying it in any substantial way.

I was too busy thinking this could be God giving me a fresh start in my relationship with men. I was thinking, maybe Leather and I could grow up together in our faith and share the journey.

Unfortunately, I was only going on what I saw, felt, and heard while spending time with him. I saw all the things we had in common. I saw he was clean and sober, attending his recovery meetings, spending quality time with his family, keeping his job going, and always looking great. I saw how popular he was with his friends and family, how easy going and fun he was to be around, and how intelligent and resourceful he was. He knew lots of people, from auto mechanics to the dentist.

When I introduced him to Chiffon, she liked him, and he liked her. He established a great relationship with her. His son, who lived in Greensboro, N.C., came down for a visit. I chose the name Khaki for his son. When Khaki arrived, both Chiffon and I fell for him. He was a great kid with a personality like his dad's. He and Chiffon quickly became instant buddies, mainly because they both had no siblings. From that visit forward, the four of us grew closer and closer. Today Chiffon and Khaki consider themselves sister and brother. Khaki has also been adopted into our extended family in Morganton.

When God showed me some early signs of Leather's immaturity and irresponsibility, I minimized them. When his rental payments began being late or were not made in full, I had to address it as I would any resident, but I did not look at it as a sign of his inability to budget his money or lack of self-control in spending. I wrote it off as needing a better paying job. God was trying to show me what

Leather's weak areas were, but I wasn't ready for that reality. I was heading for a wreck.

After a few months, Leather was talking about marriage and wasn't keeping his intentions a secret. I pushed my thoughts of those weak areas God had shown me into the back of my mind. Remember, I was good at denial.

As time passed, the residents in recovery in the building became aware of our relationship. We had been open and visible in our interactions. One day, I got a call from the Stewards, the married couple in recovery on the Spiritual Committee. They wanted to meet with me. I agreed to sit down with them.

At that meeting, both the husband and the wife shared that they did not think Leather was ready to marry anyone. They had known Leather for years in the recovery community and shared with me that his record of failed attempts to stay clean and sober was numerous. They plainly said, "Leather had a long history of relapses and advised me not to marry him.

They said they believed he would end up turning my life and Chiffon's life upside down. I had gotten to know them well, and I knew them to be sincere and caring people. I could not ignore what they had said.

I had doubts and concerns about the risk of marrying Leather. Instead of taking all of my worries to Jesus and asking Him, I

196

continued to try to figure it out myself. I was still doing the driving. Jesus was in the front seat next to me, but I was still deciding the turns and stops. I would not relinquish control of the car.

I told myself that Leather and I had a chance of making it work. I was not in love with him, as I had been with my first love, Suede. But despite the tremendous challenges that came with Leather, he was more likable than any man I have ever met. Until this day, he was the most easy-going, good-natured man I've met *and* he loved to dance!

I kept looking at the potential I thought he and I had for a good life together and ignoring the negative signs from God and from the caring people God sent to warn me. I decided to take the risk; I kept on driving.

Not long after that, Leather called me all excited. I was at my desk working. He wanted to see me right away. I told him I was stuck with doing some necessary entries and could not meet him. He insisted that he had something to say to me that could not wait. He was on his way back to the building and asked me to meet him at the elevator.

I met him at the elevator, and he had this big smile on his face; there was a closet next door to the elevator. He asked me to unlock it and pulled me inside. He said he had something for me. He pulled out a velvet ring box, said, let's get married and opened the box.

Inside the box was the most beautiful diamond ring wedding set I had ever seen. My eyes were saying yes, and my mouth said yes, so I went with yes! My feelings and emotions took over at that moment, and I rode off that wave of emotions until the day I said, "*I Do!*" a few months later.

Our outing in the park had occurred about a year before the proposal in the closet. The closet was not the most romantic location I could have envisioned, but that ring was gorgeous. Leather had good taste indeed! I had no idea how he could have afforded that ring with his income, but I didn't spend too much time thinking about it. I didn't want to burst my bubble.

Leather and I were married by the pastor at Oakhurst Baptist Church on April 30, 1994. Chiffon, Denim, his wife, and her daughter were present for our ceremony.

I have been married three times, but I have never had "a real husband." None of my choices were like the husbands described in the Bible, who were a protector and a provider for his family and loved his wife like Christ loved the church. None of my choices of men had any ability to be anyone's husband. They were all emotionally broken men who were making no effort to get repaired.

On the other side of the coin, out of my three marriages, only one man had a real wife like the wife of the Bible. Today, I can see what happened. Three times, I said, *"I Do!"* Three times I stood in churches before God and made wifely vows to three different men without any real understanding of the vows I had taken before God. I could not be anyone's wife. When I married Leather, I was still an emotionally damaged woman, but I had a desire to be repaired, and I had found the help I needed to do it. My support was God and my relationship with Jesus Christ.

Before giving my life to Jesus Christ, I walked out of two marriages. When those marriages got tough, and what I was hoping for was not happening, my three-tier solution was separation, divorce, and keep it moving. My focus throughout both of those marriages was how I felt, what I wanted, and what I needed.

God was already using the women of Al-Anon, the biblical "bad girls," and "hurting women" to promote my emotional healing process. These were the first two pieces God would use, but a third piece was required. God's final work would complete my "total deliverance package." My marriage to Leather would be that last piece. The trials and storms of my marriage to Leather would be the environment where I would grab hold of God and His Word in a way that would renew my mind, reshape my character, and change my identity.

I went into the marriage, still at the wheel and having wrecks, but I came out relaxing in the back seat. During those nineteen years, I became *His Girl*, Spirit, mind, body, and soulfully!!

This is what I learned from all three of my marriages. A messed-up person causes messes, and a damaged person causes damage, and hurting people hurt other people. I was all of these.

When two broken people marry and divorce, unhealed hurts, unmet needs, and unresolved issues are the marriage's destroyers. The selfish acts, self-centered behavior, addictions, infidelity, financial dysfunction, emotional and mental pain that occurs are not the causes of the divorce. The divorces were just an off-spring of the brokenness in the spouses. Divorce is the fruit that often grows in a marriage when one or both people are broken and refuse to acknowledge and deal with their brokenness.

I blamed my first two exes for the marriages failing. After years in my relationship with Christ and His Word, I stopped placing all the blame on my exes. I recognized my flaws and defects of character and took responsibility for my part. My desire to know the real truth of what happened in those marriages did not come until years after I gave my life to Jesus Christ. When I became willing to look at myself in the scenarios, God began revealing the whole truth of my brokenness little by little. The process was only beginning when I became distracted by my third husband, Leather.

I was blind to the reality of what my choice to ignore God would cost me. Leather and I settled in at GlenCastle in my unit, which was much larger than his, but it was still too cramped for the three of us.

We were trying to figure out our options when we decided that it was a good time for a quick trip home to Morganton. Leather was excited, and so was Chiffon and I. One of our favorite things to do became road trips. Leather was a great driver, and he was a lot of fun when traveling, especially when visiting family and friends. We decided to go to Morganton for the weekend since we were officially a family.

It would be the first of several fun family trips home to Morganton that would be sprinkled here and there throughout the years of our marriage. Two of my favorites were a camping trip and a beach trip. Both Chiffon and Khaki still like to look at the pictures from our camping and beach trips in North Carolina. Family events in North Carolina often included my mother, Denim, Lace, Satin, and all their kids. Those were times when Leather was in his element and when we enjoyed him the most. He loved it when we did things as a family.

Everyone who met Leather in Morganton fell for him instantly. My mother and both my sisters liked him. I introduced him to all my extended family and friends, and the response was unanimous, he was a hit. The amazing thing was that he wasn't even trying; he was just himself. In my mind, seeing that I wasn't the only one caught up under his spell made my wrong decision more understandable but did not change the reality of what lay ahead.

When we returned, it was back to seriously looking for a place to live in our current neighborhood. I didn't want Chiffon to have to change schools. She was in middle school at that time and doing very well.

We were looking at what we could afford when I began to see the side of Leather that I had been avoiding. He didn't seem to have a handle on what his monthly expenses were, which was troubling. We made the plan to save the amount of money he would typically pay as rent to create the savings for us to move. I assumed that Leather was doing that until the time came to utilize those funds for our move. He did not mention that he wasn't saving as we had agreed. It was a surprise I would get when it was time for us to move.

Nancy, my boss at Charis, knew we had gotten married and were living in my apartment until we could find a larger place to live. I had gotten an okay from her to move out of the building. We made a plan. I would continue to go into the office at my regular work hours each day. We identified Mr. Stewart as a resident who could be trusted to keep watch over the building at night.

God was still opening doors, even in my disobedience. I got a call from Nancy a few weeks later saying the Charis Board of Directors had decided to make Interim Housing a community for recovering addicts and their families. The two duplexes would become a recovery community for families. I thought that was a great idea and told her that some families at GlenCastle were ready for an opportunity like that. She said that was why she was calling.

She wanted to offer Leather and I the opportunity to move to Interim Housing as the lead family in the recovery community. She thought that Leather could function as a support person for the men and that I could begin a Women's Prayer and support group one night per week. I told her that her idea sounded like a perfect fit for us and that I would call her back after talking to Leather. He also loved the idea. Just like that, God solved our housing dilemma while I remained in denial about my disobedience.

Nancy set our rent at a very modest rate, which was a huge blessing. It was apparent that she was trying to be as supportive of our family as possible. God used Nancy in many ways to bless my family and me over the years at GlenCastle.

We moved to Interim Housing, but Leather had failed to save the funds for the move. The amount he had saved would not even cover the first month's rent. Leather's excuse was that he was still paying on what he owed on my rings. He knew that would stop my questions and leave me feeling partially responsible, and it worked.

That would be the first of numerous financial problems he would leave on my plate that I would have to try to clean up in the years ahead of us. It was the beginning of numerous years spent on failed and frustrating attempts to communicate with him about money. It was becoming clear to me that neither one of us was ready for a marital relationship. I was disappointed and frustrated, and he just wanted things to be easy and fun.

If I had been ready for marriage, God's way, I would have been attentive to what God showed me about Leather and backed out of the relationship. If I had looked closely enough or long enough, I would have seen that God was not finished with Leather or with me. We both had a long way to go before being ready for marriage. I followed my feelings and thoughts like a little girl in her dream world. Too bad the dream would be over so soon.

As I got to spend time with Leather's mother and aunt, I saw and heard from them how the addiction began and how Leather had been able to spend almost twenty-five years of his life fluctuating between brief sobriety and relapse. At family gatherings, I was able to piece together the story of Leather's family life.

Atlanta was home for His mother and her two sons. Leather was the youngest and was favored by his mother. With outstanding athletic ability as a high school football quarterback, he had received multiple offers for football scholarships by his senior year at Grady High School in the City of Atlanta. Then the tragedy happened.

While working on the high-school newspaper, his throwing hand got caught in the printing press and was severely damaged.

After several surgical procedures, doctors saved his hand, but it was left barely usable and deformed. Leather's dreams of being a college quarterback ended with that tragic accident. His addiction to drugs began with using pain killers during his surgeries and recovery. The pain of losing the use of his hand and losing his dream set in motion a lifelong battle with addiction that he never won.

His mother's response to his tragic loss was to overcompensate and attempt to make everything alright by buying him a new car his senior year, by dressing him in the finest of clothing, and by trying to give him anything he said he wanted. This was her way of easing his pain. Her love for him and sorrow over what happened to him engaged her in years and years of misguided attempts to make up for what he had lost. She was a significant financial resource behind the money that kept coming in for his drug purchases over the years.

Because his mother remained healthy and strong into her seventies, she continued to work full-time up until a few days before her unexpected death. She became unable to resist giving Leather money when he showed up at her door. Sadly, she stayed trapped in that pattern until her end.

Leather was seventeen when he began using addictive drugs. One of the recovery community theories is that whatever your age is when you start using an addictive substance, it becomes the age where you begin again once you achieve sobriety. In other words, Leather's developmental growth into maturity stalled out when he started using drugs. He was a spoiled seventeen-year-old on the inside. He was immature, irresponsible, and self-centered. I always felt like I was the only adult in our marriage.

At this point, he had almost two-years of clean time. He joined in with Chiffon and I in attending Beulah Cathedral Church and won everyone's hearts there too. He was naturally amiable and seemed to enjoy all the fellowship types of functions. He willingly participated in Sunday Services and never complained, but I never saw any real desire to grow deeper in his relationship with Jesus Christ or utilize his Bible. He seemed content with just being saved and baptized.

From the beginning, we struggled with finances. I was very disciplined in that area, but he was like a kid when paying bills and spending. I came into the marriage with an A-1 credit rating, and I ended up having to endure a foreclosure and bankruptcy.

Leather's first relapse came in our second year of marriage and happened about ten months after moving to Interim Housing. We were supposed to be the lead family in the recovery community, not the recovery community's relapsed family. The news of Leather's relapse spread fast in the Interim Housing community, at GlenCastle, and I am sure at Charis and FCS.

While I continued working at GlenCastle and living at Interim Housing, Nancy continued to be a source of support for me. We communicated regarding Leather's relapse and its effect on the residents in the recovery community where we were living. She showed a great deal of trust in my judgment as I tried to make the right decisions as Leather's wife as well as for the recovery families living in Interim Housing. I did what I had to do for the residents and Leather.

I immediately called Leather's Narcotics Anonymous Sponsor, Ed Williams, to let him know. He talked with Leather and strongly recommended that he go into treatment directly. I tried to get Leather to follow his advice. After about two weeks and a lot of pressure from Ed and I, Leather half-heartedly went back into treatment in the men's recovery program at Oakhurst Baptist Church.

When he completed the three-month treatment plan, I asked if he could prolong his stay a few weeks to give me more time to prepare Chiffon and me for his return. I also wanted to inform the adults in the recovery community. The recovery residents at Interim Housing had shown me lots of support, and when Leather returned, they were encouraging and supportive of him.

I had continued to meet with the women weekly, did my best to be candid about what had happened and how Leather was doing in recovery. When Leather returned, he had to rebuild and restructure his relationship with the men since he had less clean time than any of them. Things felt rather uncomfortable between them for a while, but honest communication between them and Leather seemed to have helped. In time, everyone adjusted, but things were never the same, at least from my perspective.

There would be two more relapses where he returned to heroin during the first ten years of our marriage. Each relapse episode became more severe with a   longer duration and more damaging results for us all.

The first relapse was his shortest, but for Chiffon and I, everything changed. It was just like the Stewart's had predicted. Our lives were turned upside down. As the shock, anxiety, and disappointment gradually subsided, it left the residue of "when will it happen again" and a complete lack of trust in Leather. These were the leftovers that would remain.

Our financial situation had gotten worse while he was in treatment. I was grateful that Leather was good at finding work. God had gifted him in so many unique ways. We had fallen further behind financially, but his personality and skills always gained him entry to a job somewhere. The problem was never a lack of ability, job opportunities, or earning capacity. It was still the lack of maturity and self-discipline, a lack of desire to face his internal issues, and a lack of spiritual growth.

After the first relapse occurred, I knew what I needed to do. I made a big decision. I repented and asked God to forgive me for not backing off when he showed me Leather's weaknesses. I regretted and asked God's forgiveness for not listening to the married couple's pleas on the Spiritual Committee when He sent them. While I was at it, I repented and asked God to forgive me for becoming sexually intimate with Leather before we were married. I took responsibility for all of my disobedience and sin and the difficult situation I found myself in.

I decided I would not walk out this time. I decided to face the mess I had made by my disobedience. There had been too many divorces in my past. I saw my history of divorce as a family curse. I decided to break the curse of divorce on my life and not leave a legacy of three broken marriages to Chiffon. She deserved better than that. I wanted Chiffon to know that with God on your side, you can survive the trials that will come in marriage.

I decided to ask God to show me how to be a "real wife" to Leather. I decided that I would stay and finish the marriage if God would help me. I told God I wanted to finish it this time, no matter what it would take on my part.

God kept me and made me a way through Leather's three relapse periods. God kept me sane, made provisions when needed, kept me faithful to my ministry assignments, helped me take care of Chiffon, and kept me faithful throughout our marriage. Who else but God could do that?

I began asking God each day how to make it through. I allowed the Holy Spirit to guide me. While Leather was in recovery, I called and asked him to move into Chiffon's bedroom when he returned. I told him Chiffon could use the downstairs bedroom when she came home for visits. I turned my bedroom into my sanctuary and prayer closet; my bedroom became my place to spiritually and emotionally refuel. It was my place of respite, quiet. My bedroom became "operation central" to get directions on navigating the tumultuous times ahead of me.

Somewhere after Leathers' return home, I began taking a closer look at the role I was playing as his wife. The understanding I was getting from the Bible was that as his wife, I should be his *helper* as he pursues ways of being the protector and provider for our family. The problem was that I had not seen Leather actively involved in any activities that showed him to be focused on protecting or providing for our family at that point. So, I was confused about what being his helper meant.

The Bible did not give examples or define what things a wife should do to help her husband. I met with my pastor but recognized there was no way he could understand what I was facing, but I began trying to be more encouraging. I looked for opportunities to help Leather succeed at work, and I intentionally became more supportive.

Leather found his dream job. He was hired by Positive Growth, Inc., a large non-profit organization that served troubled boys by providing them with a boy's home (residential program). Positive Growth was designed to help the boys succeed in every area of their lives. The Positive Growth housing could accommodate about twenty-five boys ranging in age from about twelve to eighteen.

Leather loved working there and was getting an opportunity to use his administrational skills and impact the boys. His salary was adequate and could have provided the extra income he needed to stabilize us financially, but that never happened.

That was when he began pressuring me or rather, "wearing me down" until I gave in to co-signing with him to buy a nearly new Volvo. I tried hard to persuade him to buy something less expensive without any success. I reminded him that I already had a car payment of my own. I told him if he failed to keep the payments going, the car would have to go back.

I knew my credit rating would be at risk if he failed to make his payments. He had no credit history, and my credit rating was A-1. He swore and swore that he would keep the payments going and that I did not need to worry. UGH!! What a giant size mistake that was!! That was not the right kind of help for Leather.

A few years passed. We were still living at Interim Housing. I served as the Chaplain at GlenCastle and continued providing the

Fit for the Kingdom After School Boy's Club. Leather had begun interacting with the boys in the club from time to time. It seemed to be mutually rewarding to him and the boys. Chiffon was away in college and doing well.

At home, Leather and I were still having significant conflicts over paying our bills. If he had managed his spending more responsibly, his salary would have been adequate. But instead, his spending escalated on clothes, shoes, and jewelry as he wanted to look the part of a Volvo owner. He could never provide his portion of our household expenses, and he had added credit card debt. The promises kept coming to do better next pay period, but the struggle with finances never ended. I remained the frustrated and struggling adult in that area while he enjoyed his pretend life.

I wanted to be a good wife but felt like things were so far out of balance. I needed to know what kind of help and how much help to provide. I had learned about the term "enabler" from my Al-Anon meetings. An enabler is a person in the addict's life whose actions enable the addict to continue using. His mother had been his enabler all of his adult life. I felt like he was my teenage son, not my husband.

I wanted to know if I might be an enabler in Leather's life. I shared my concerns with my Al-Anon mentors, and they had no simple principle or rule to apply as a godly wife. Situations got complicated when two people were married, lived together, and had an on-going relapse problem. My mentors shared from their early experiences with their husbands, who had many years of sobriety. Leather was a unique case.

They both agreed that sometimes "tough love" has to be applied even in a marriage situation to bring about change and growth. My stress level was going up, and my emotional wellbeing level was going down. I had to do something.

I knew about "tough love" being used successfully with teenagers. I remembered that Leather was seventeen when his addiction began. I also knew that Leather had not decided to build on his relationship with God. I prayed and felt peaceful about moving forward.

I thought, "It might be time for some "tough love." I also started encouraging him to spend some time with Pastor Ron, whom he had known for years when they associated as addicts. I suggested that he attend the weekly Bible Study at the church being taught by another man who liked Leather and had shown an interest in connecting with him.

I continued praying and asking God to show me the right responses and give me the ability to carry them out. I knew God wanted Leather to become the man He created him to be. I also knew He wanted me to succeed as a wife and victoriously finish my marriage. I just needed God to show me the way to do it, and He did!

Our financial situation didn't change, but I began to change my response to Leathers' broken promises and irresponsibility. I let him know that I would no longer be trying to cover the shortfalls on the bills he was supposed to pay. I told him that I was prepared to do without whatever did not get paid.

In response, he began asking me to lend him funds when he had his shortfalls. He was promising to repay me his next pay period. I tried that. It ended up with him owing me money that I never received back.

I stopped lending him money, and sure enough, utilities sometimes got turned off. Chiffon was away at school, and I thanked God for that. I learned to trust in God. I reminded myself of how I got there. So, I knew to light a few candles, add some extra blankets, tune out what others might think of our dark apartment, and find peace in my sanctuary when Leather gave me the silent treatment.

When the second relapse happened, we were still living at Interim Housing, which was still a recovery community. After the first relapse, I had become more attentive to his behavior during his free time. I did notice a change in his routines but did not know it was a signal of a relapse. I had no idea what triggered his relapse, which was the first question Ed asked me when I called to let him know.

Ed sounded frustrated and discouraged by the news, but he immediately contacted Leather. I told Ed that Leather could not return to Interim Housing if he regained his sobriety this time. I told him I believed a time of separation would be good for both of us.

Feeling both dread and embarrassment, I contacted Nancy to tell her about the second relapse. I informed her that Leather's sponsor was trying to get him back in treatment, but I had decided that I needed a time of separation. I let her know that Leather would not be coming back to Interim Housing.

I had no thoughts of divorce. When Ed told Leather what I had said about not returning to Interim Housing, the phone started ringing off the hook. I told him I did not want a divorce and had no intentions of seeking a divorce, but I needed some separation time.

One day, I headed across the parking lot into a neighborhood drug store when I ran into Leather by surprise. I was caught off guard and shocked by his unkept appearance. His clothes did not fit, he had lost a lot of weight, and his shoes and socks were filthy. It made me feel sad to see what his relapsed life looked like. We chatted a minute; he asked about Chiffon. I told him to call Ed. He said he would. I walked away, wondering if He would ever decide he deserved more.

By this time, Leather had missed a few payments on the Volvo. The dealership began to hound me about the missed payments. The

215

dealership person said they would repossess the car if the payments were not caught up immediately. If that could not happen soon, he recommended that we voluntarily surrender it. He explained that a "voluntary surrender" of the car would look better on my credit report than a "repossession." I agreed. I was overwhelmed by the financial mess I was facing. Even a small concession like that sounded good.

The dreaded day had come; I wasn't sure what I could do. Leather had the Volvo. I hadn't seen the car in a couple of months. But I was more than ready to surrender it. I contacted Leather, who was still using heroin, and tried to reason with him. He said he wasn't about to give them his car. He was adamant about trying to keep the car. I did not see any other options. My hands were tied.

A couple of weeks later, he came by unexpectedly to pick up something he left in the apartment. I noticed that the car was not in the driveway. When he left, I noticed he was walking across the yard and headed up into the neighborhood. I followed him from a distance and saw him get in the Volvo. It was parked a few blocks away on a neighborhood street where he had hidden it to prevent repossession.

I decided that if it were there the next morning, I would drive it out to the dealership and turn it in. I told Chiffon about my plan and that I would need her to follow me out there. I don't remember praying about this decision. Looking back on it, I was mostly responding to the stress I was feeling, but God kept me because nothing went wrong.

The next morning, I got the spare key that I had, grabbed my purse, and we headed to where I had seen it parked. It was there. I was afraid and very nervous that Leather might come walking down that street and catch me, and I didn't want that to happen. I got in as quickly as I could, and we headed to the dealership.

I was not looking forward to another embarrassing situation, but I pulled up to the dealership, got out, and bravely walked up to the first salesman I saw. I quickly introduced myself, gave a brief explanation, handed him the key, got in the car with Chiffon, and we headed home. Both Chiffon and I were wiped out after that escapade.

I didn't even want to think about what would happen when Leather found the car gone, but it was all I could think about all the way home and up until it happened. I thank God that the confrontation was by phone because he was furious. He "went off," and then he "went off" some more!!! Thank God, he was not a physically abusive man, but he was a pro at yelling and creating a big dramatic scene, even on the phone. I quietly took what was coming to me and reminded him that he promised me that this would never happen.

Weeks later, He finally followed Ed's guidance and went into another substance abuse treatment facility. When he came out several months later, he moved back into GlenCastle. I was no longer working there.

Our marriage had endured job losses, income losses, and failed attempts to stay clean, and devastating financial setbacks. Leather's addiction drove him to take things from our home to sell, to empty our joint bank accounts, and max our credit cards to buy items to sell so that he could continue to buy heroin.

Our marriage and family life were turned upside down each time by the chaos, anxiety, emotional trauma, and financial stress that came with Leather's addiction. There were sleepless nights and stressful days. Every area of my life and Chiffon's life were affected, while Leather never seemed to notice.

Chiffon was still at home when the first relapse occurred, and all I can remember was that it was God's presence with us that got us to throw it. I do remember her being afraid he might overdose, and honestly, I was too. That is the greatest fear when dealing with heroin addiction.

Thankfully, Chiffon was off at college during the other two relapses. I asked God to protect Chiffon from the negative effects of all the chaos, pain, and anxiety that my decision had brought on us.

As far as I knew, Leather was still living at GlenCastle. There wasn't much communication between us for months. I kept in contact with Ed. I got a call from Ed about six months later letting me know Leather had relapsed a third time.

During that time, Chiffon came home for a couple of weeks during a summer break. It was just what I needed. Chiffon and I got to spend some quality time together.

Somehow stories of the good times we had spent with Leather started popping up. One year at Christmas, while Leather was still working full-time at Positive Growth, he found an older model Volvo (of course) and managed to save money to buy it as a Christmas gift for Chiffon. He put a big red bow on it and had it waiting for her when she came home from college for the holidays. She was totally surprised and thrilled. It was hard to say which one of them had the bigger smile on their faces. He was as excited and as happy as Chiffon about being able to do that. We agreed that was our best Christmas holiday.

My communications with Khaki and with Leather's mother and aunt were on-going throughout our marriage. They stopped considering Leather a reliable source of information. They depended on me to keep them informed on how he was doing. I often became the bearer of bad news and disappointing updates. It was a role I would have gladly given up.

However, Leather's addiction created a unique bond between us as his family and there were good times of family fellowship whether Leather was with us clean and sober or absent because of a relapse.

One time, Leather drove his mother, two aunts, Chiffon and I to Ohio for their family reunion. He made that trip so much fun for us. He was so patient and good natured with his van load of girls. He catered to us no matter how loud we talked or how many pit-stops we asked him to make. He made the trip there and back a pleasure.

Just weeks after Ed's call about Leather's third relapse, I got a call from Leather's aunt. She was calling to let me know that his mother had been rushed to the hospital by ambulance. She asked if I could contact Leather and tell him to come to the hospital as soon as possible. She said it looked very serious. As far as I knew, Leather was still in treatment. I called Ed knowing that he would probably be able to reach him more quickly. When I got to the hospital, the emergency room staff were frantically trying to save her. By the time Leather got there, she was gone.

When Leather arrived and was given the news, he fell completely apart in the hallway of the emergency room. There was no consoling him for what seemed like hours. When the family was invited in to see her body, he just kept walking around the room saying no, refusing to accept the reality of what was right in front of his eyes.

Later on, a couple of men in the family, were finally able to take him back to his recovery center.

There were concerns in the family that he would leave recovery and go out and start using again that night, but that didn't happen. Leather showed up for his mother's funeral clean and sober and accompanied by Ed.

I was hopeful that the addiction cycle was broken from his life forever. The main reason I was hopeful was because his mother passed while he was in treatment during another relapse. Her death hit him really hard especially since he had just recently relapsed again. I think Leather always thought that he would have time to give her what her heart longed for which was to see him clean and sober and living a stable and productive life. His time to do that in her lifetime had run out.

I hoped that her death would awaken him to the reality of the damage he was doing to the people who loved him. As I sat beside Leather at her funeral service, we all listened to her pastor say that he had spoken to his mother earlier that week at her home. She had suddenly gotten sick.

Prior to that week, she was still going to work full-time at a daycare center. She had no major health problems. Then unexpectedly, she suddenly developed a blood clot that went to her lungs and took her life.

221

Her pastor went on to say that during that visit he asked her, "What was it?" "He said, her tearful answer was "Leather". That was a hard truth for Leather to hear, but he needed to hear the truth. It was a truth that he would have to live with. It was a truth that every close family member already knew.

Months later, he finished his treatment and left the recovery center. To my knowledge, he never returned to using heroin or any type of addictive substance again. But there is more to the story.

He was trying to get back on track. Leather called me when he secured his job back at Positive Growth. Obviously, the impact he made while he was there was significant. I was happy for him and congratulated him on his return to work. We began talking more often. He told me he wanted us to get back together and was going to find us a house. I didn't respond to what he said, but let him do the talking. He said he would let me know when he found a house.

When I heard from him the next time, he had found a condo for rent with an option to buy. It belonged to the man who owned and operated Positive Growth.

Leather was very excited as he described it and the rental amount sounded reasonable. My response was, "I am not going to sign anything. I told him if he wanted us to get back together, he would have to rent it, sign the lease and leave me out of it. He said okay, he was going to get it done.

In my prayer closet, I said, "Okay Lord". I'll go, only if you go with me". I felt peace. I knew God would be with me.

He succeeded in securing the condo with plans to buy it a year later. We moved in. It was an attractive small two-bedroom unit with two full bathrooms. It had a beautiful little sunroom on the front side. Chiffon had graduated from college and was living on her own, so it was a perfect fit for us and in a great location.

I loved the condo, but knew Leather was prone to relapses and at best unpredictable. Feeling insecure about everything related to Leather had become a way of life for me. The only security I knew I could count on was found in my relationship with Jesus Christ. He was my strength, protector and my source in all things.

I thought Leather had taken care of everything when we were allowed to move in. We had been in the condo about two months, when he unexpectedly came home with the lease saying that the owner was insisting that I sign it. Shocked and upset, I said no. Leather had led me to believe that he had done everything the way we initially agreed. He was supposed to take care of everything and leave me out of it. He never mentioned the lease again and neither did I.

About a year later, I was searching through our bedroom drawers for something and came across an envelope that was stuffed in the back of one of the drawers. A copy of the lease was inside it. I opened it to find out that Leather had forged my signature on the lease. To say I was upset, would be putting it mildly. When I confronted him, he said the owner was pressuring him for my signature saying he would not rent to us without my signature, so he signed my name on the lease. I just walked away. Later on, I told him what I thought about him forging my signature and breaking another promise to me, then I let it go. It was time to purchase the condo and amazingly, we were on track to do that.

But that same day, I also saw something else that got my attention. There was a small stack of lottery tickets on Leathers night stand. I had seen some around before over the past year. He and some of his family members had gotten fond of playing the Georgia Lottery. It seemed to be something they enjoyed, but I had doubts about whether or not it was a good idea for Leather to start playing the lottery. I did not share my concerns with him at that time, but that day stood out for some reason. I didn't know that it was God giving me a preview of things to come.

Leather was still clean and sober and had found an additional side job where he was earning some additional income. We were trying to save the amount we would need for the down payment and closing cost.

We made it to the point of buying the condo. We went into the attorneys' office to do the closing. We arrived and were seated at the table with the owner and all the necessary paper work when I got blindsided by a totally unexpected, grossly important detail.

As the paperwork was being presented, I found out that I had been entered as the person primarily responsible for the repayment of the loan. I was shocked. I could not believe what I was hearing and asked the attorney to repeat what he had said. I asked what that meant exactly and found out that basically it meant that if anything went wrong with the mortgage loan being repaid, I would have the primary responsibility.

I looked at Leather and could tell that he knew about this. I let them know that I was not aware of that situation and was not prepared to sign in that capacity. They looked at Leather as if to say "really man"? I was so embarrassed, again!   I wanted to tell them I needed some time to choke my husband to death, but instead I told them I needed some time to talk with my husband.

I tried to control myself when we got in the car and the only way I felt I could do that was to say nothing at all. Leather knew not to say one word to me. Thankfully, we were not far from home. When I got to my bedroom, I just broke down and cried. I told God I was doing my best. I had forgiven Leather and let go of so much stuff, but the blows just kept on coming and coming. I needed God to tell me what to do. I was exhausted with Leather and his manipulative and hurtful antics where I always came out on the losing end.

I was exhausted emotionally and mentally and even felt spiritually drained. They said they would like to finish the transaction within forty-eight hours. I fell asleep hoping God would give me a clear direction the next day.

The next day, I confronted Leather and asked why he didn't tell me about what was going to happen before I got there. He said, because he knew I would say no. That meant that he deliberately set me up hoping that doing it publicly would pressure me into signing. That was a painful reality that I was already too familiar with.

He began his arguments with his lack of good credit. I told him my credit was a wreck too since we got married. I did not know how they determined I was a good risk. I had twice as much debt as I had income by this point. He said what he always said, he will pay the mortgage payment, he will take care of it. I said, I remember your promises to do blah…blah…blah. I said, I have heard your promises many times before. The problem is you never managed to keep any of them. I said, "I had no reason to believe you would keep this one." He countered with, "just give me one more chance, please. This time it is going to work out".

His next point was he had a good fulltime job and the side job was bringing in money too. And his final point was, "Where will we go if we don't purchase the condo?" He said, "The owner was ready to sale it and if we didn't buy it, we would have to move out and find another place to live".

By this time, I was exhausted again. I went back to my bedroom for a little peace and quiet time.

While all of this was going on at home, I was in graduate school, finishing the writing of the curriculum and establishing the missionary academy. Thank God, I was enjoying graduate school and writing the curriculum. I was in my element and excited about recruiting some students. From the beginning, ministering to women was a place where I felt at home. My life was enriched as I served the women God sent. Things in that arena were good. God knew I needed a positive outlet and some balance.

I began thinking about how much I loved the condo and the idea of moving again was not appealing at all. I also thought, what if Leather retained his sobriety and could make it work this time. I thought, maybe the loss of his mother caused a change on the inside. I thought what if we could become homeowners instead of renters?

I decided that was enough of my thinking. What I really needed was to hear what God had to say. I remembered the Volvo ordeal I got myself into. I needed God to tell me if I should sign my name on that mortgage agreement. This time I was asking Him. Should I take that risk? That was my question for God.

I prayed for the answer, read my Bible looking for the answer and listened for the answer from the Holy Spirit inside me. The only response I felt sure I was getting from God was that "He was with me. He would never leave me or forsake me". I knew that had been true from the very beginning. God had taken very good care of Chiffon and I, but I was hoping for a specific yes or no answer.

I began looking back over my marriage to Leather and I could clearly see that God had never failed me. In the worst moments of it, God always got me through. Even when I was disobedient, He lovingly forgave me and allowed me to learn and grow in my relationship with Him.

So okay, I knew God had my back. The forty-eight hours were almost up. Time had run out. I decided to take the risk and give Leather another opportunity to get it right. I thought, "Maybe, this time he would do it". It felt like a now or never moment to me.

In the midst of Leather's failures to manage his addiction, the incredible waste of money on drugs, the chaos, anxiety, embarrassment and my ruined credit, God balanced the scale with the amazing blessings of having Chiffon and my family and being able to do meaningful ministry serving women. Leather's family and Khaki were also a source of joy. I was healthy, strong and active. I also belonged to a great church.

I felt God guiding me towards focusing my attention and energy on the positive components of my life and to trust Him with everything else. God awakened me to savoring the positives and good times in my life. He reminded me to remember the good sides of my life when the difficult times came. Once I discovered what mattered the most, life stopped throwing me off balance so easily. I had found a focal point.

We purchased the condo. Although heroin never became a part of his life again, the addiction transferred from heroin to gambling. That stack of lottery tickets I saw on his night stand was a preview of things to come. The Georgia Lottery became his new drug of choice and became just as destructive to our marriage, finances and family as heroine.

He continued to work both jobs, but his addiction to gambling destroyed every chance of us holding on to our home. With income from both jobs, Leather continually poured his money into playing the lottery. I was literally finding plastic bags of lottery tickets hidden around the house. I found them in his pants, jacket and coat pockets and all through his car. Leather's gambling went completely out of control. All his bills piled up, utilities were turned off and finally the mortgage payments were being missed in spite of his adequate income. I let the process take its course. We lost our home. The condo ended up in foreclosure about five years after we purchased it.

Looking back on it all now, I don't regret signing that mortgage. Leather got his final chance to get it right. Leather was drug free, but still trapped by the "enemy within" that had fueled his addiction to heroin and that would continue to fuel his addiction to gambling until the end of his life.

In my third marriage, I learned to trust God for real! I knew I would be okay because God was with me. Although it led to my financial collapse, I still had the things that mattered the most. God did what He said He would do. He never left me. He continued to make me a way through. Leather rented us another house that belonged to the condo owner. That house became our final home together.

I was able to remain in ministry during this time due to the faithful giving of the supporters God had given me and later by drawing my Social Security. Chiffon was engaged to be married to a good man and had found a job she loved working for a large non-profit organization that served children and teens in the inner city of Atlanta.

Khaki was working and going to college part-time at home in Greensboro, N.C. Leather's favorite aunt was still doing well. Everyone was really hoping that this time, Leather would get it right. Everyone was disappointed again and sorry that it did not work out for my sake.

Not long after we moved into the rental house, Leather's health began to deteriorate. First, he was diagnosed with hypertension and shortly after that with diabetes in spite of him being below the normal weight for a man his height. He began taking medication for hypertension and ended up being placed on Insulin a couple months after his diabetes diagnosis.

I felt as if I was caught up in a whirlwind with Leather's continued gambling, the foreclosure, moving out of the condo, all topped off with Leather's new health problems. I was going through the motions physically, without any connection to my emotional side and very little time for keeping myself strong spiritually. I was doing what had to be done each day. Needless to say, I was exhausted, again.

It was a couple more months before things settled down enough for me to even think about where I was in the midst of all of this. I felt like I needed to step out of the middle of everything and just rest for a while. Thankfully, there were two bedrooms and two full baths upstairs in the house we rented. I needed a get-away for real, but I could only afford a trip upstairs to my sanctuary (bedroom) which I had finally gotten in order. Whew!! What a blessing an at-home sanctuary can be to a weary woman who needs to fall into the arms of Jesus. That is exactly what I did for about two days.

I knew I was okay physically and I was so grateful to have quality time to reconnect with God spiritually. The spiritual reconnection renewed my strength so that I could address the other areas of my life. My financial situation was a "jacked up mess" with the return of the Volvo, the foreclosure and all my other unpaid bills. I was considering filing for bankruptcy and did so later on.

I felt I was okay mentally since I was not planning on doing any harm to Leather, even though a judge would probably have let me go free.

Emotionally, I wasn't doing so good. That was my area of concern. There was always an amount of emotional hurt I had to deal with throughout the marriage, but the emotional hurt became toxic after Leather stopped using heroin, and then picked up gambling and allowed it take over.

When the gambling continued to escalate, I felt like his level of disregard for me as a person reached beyond my emotional tolerance level. I tried sharing how I was feeling and pleaded with him to get some help. I asked him again about reaching out to Pastor Ron or the man at the church. In return for my efforts, I got more promises that he never kept.

Depression and crying settled in on me. I started crying out to God almost daily asking for relief from what felt like spiritual warfare. I felt like I was waging war with the enemy every day in my own home.

A couple more months passed with no let up on his gambling, but Leather's blood pressure and diabetes was responding well to the medications. He was still working full time at Positive Growth.

I felt drained emotionally and physically. I asked God to give me another break from Leather and to open up a way for me to separate from him for a while. I felt totally at peace about separating for a while because emotionally, I was done. The home scene had become too much.

I started thinking. Denim was living back inside the city and had split with his wife. When I had spoken to him last, he had rented out an extra bedroom in his house to a friend in order to cut back on his household expenses. I decided to give him a call to see if anything had changed.

When I called, the friend had moved out. I explained my financial and emotional condition and as usual Denim said, "Yes, I could come stay with him". We worked out a monthly payment agreement that fit us both.

When I told Leather, I was going to go stay with Denim a while he dramatically feel-apart and begged and pleaded with me not to go. I stuck to my plan knowing I had to get myself out of that emotionally toxic environment. I moved in with Denim and Leather adjusted.

I could feel the pressure begin to subside even as I began to pack to leave. Leather called me almost every day sometimes for no real reason. I stayed available to him and kept track of his medical condition. I went by to check on him periodically. He was not living as well as before, but he was okay and he was still working and still gambling.

Almost exactly a year later, Leather called. He sounded very sick. I went over and had to take him to the emergency room. He was having problems breathing. He was admitted to the hospital and a battery of test were run to determine a diagnosis.

While he was at the hospital, I told Denim I would come back home to take care of him. I moved my things back into my bedroom at home. I could hear the Holy Spirit inside of me letting me know that this new illness was serious. God had given me a year-long break to restore me and prepare me for the final years of Leather's life.

When all the tests were completed, the doctor gave us the findings. Leather's Kidneys were shutting down and he would need to go on Dialysis three times a week. The tests also indicated that he had Congestive Heart failure. It was causing the breathing problems.

Leather was in the hospital for almost two weeks. His Dialysis treatments began while he was in the hospital along with the treatments to get the Congestive Heart Failure under control. He was put on several new medications. They wanted to have time to see how he would respond to all of these new treatments and medicines before discharging him.

I knew he would not be able to go back to work for a while and that returning to work full-time might become impossible with Dialysis three times a week. Leather and I talked and decided it would be a good idea for him to file for disability while he was still in the hospital.

I met with the hospital social worker and completed the process of applying for disability for Leather. Amazingly, he was approved about a month after he was discharged. With his disability income coming in, we were able to cover the rent each month.

On the inside, I could hear "step away from my ministry life and take care of him". I followed God's directions. I took a leave from all my ministry assignments. I had to notify my financial contributors of my need to leave ministry for an undetermined length of time to care for my husband. I had to also suspend the missionary academy classes indefinitely. These actions automatically ended any financial support I was receiving from my contributors.

When we returned home from the hospital, I talked to Leather about his salvation and his relationship with Jesus Christ. I asked him if He was sure of his salvation. He said that he was not sure and agreed to allow me to lead him in giving his life to Jesus Christ. Leather gave his life to Jesus Christ.

All in all, Leather was a good guy with unhealed hurts, unmet needs and unresolved issues that he never would give to God.

Leather never made building a relationship with Jesus Christ a priority. An intimate relationship or hunger for knowing Jesus Christ personally never developed in him.

After about twelve months, he adjusted to dialysis and his health situation stabilized briefly. For a while, he was able to go back to work part-time and I went back to doing ministry on a limited basis.

The last eighteen months of Leather's life were spent fighting the horrible combination of medical conditions that had developed including Kidney Failure, Hypertension, Diabetes, Hepatitis C, Congestive Heart Failure and finally Liver Cancer. All those years of heroin use had taken a detrimental toll on his vital organs.

It got to the point where we were spending more time in hospitals and rehab centers than at home. One of his best days in the rehab center was a day when three of his Grady High School classmates came for a visit. One or two of them were on the high school football team with him. He smiled that day! Finally, after two weeks in the hospital and six weeks in the last rehabilitation facility, hospice care was recommended.

Leather asked me to take him home. That same day, Leather told me that I had been a good wife to him and that he should have treated me much better. I told him that I really appreciated him saying that and that everything was alright. That was the last real conversation we had.

I enlisted the help of a hospice agency and took him home. He lived about two more months at home. Having him at home went much better than I expected. Being at home made visitations easier and more relaxed. His family, friends, boss, co-workers and some of our neighbors dropped by to visit with him. He got to spend time with Chiffon's two-year old son and see her baby girl once more.

Chiffon and Khaki were there with him and there for me during his final days. Leather passed at home in July of 2013. He was only sixty-two years old. God was with us every day and He kept our family gathered around him and united together through it all.

Because God was with me, I did not run away this time. I kept my vows. I did my best. I stayed by his side. The divorce curse was broken!!! God did that.

I have no regrets!! Some may say that I did not have to do all that, but I did. Some people who knew our situation were probably more than ready to hear me say, " I'm done! Enough is enough!"

What they did not know was that my staying in the marriage was just as much for me as it was for him. I told God I wanted to stay if He would see me through. God did what I asked Him to do. He made me a way through even on the days when I fell apart.

God provided me with sources of joy like Chiffon, my son-in-law, my grandchildren, my siblings and extended family, good friends, my church and my love for ministry to women. Khaki was also a blessing and a source of joy. He grew into a man his dad would be proud of. These were the most important things.

God blessed me with knowing to focus on the positive sides of my life when things got tough. I became very grateful for what I had...I realized how blessed I was. This kept anger and bitterness from taking hold of me.

Laughter and maintaining my sense of humor were also great medicine. When I needed to forgive or let go of something, I often found the strength to do it through the Holy Spirit and trusting in God. He was my way of coping, my comforter, my peace and my joy throughout the difficult times.

I found out that I had to change my prayer from *"Lord, change him"* to *"Lord, change me"*. Al-Anon taught me how to change my prayer and the guidance and support of my mentors helped me in my marriage to Leather.

The sweet rain was the blessings God used to heal me emotionally and the bitter rain was the bruising God used to mature and strengthen me spiritually. God used the blessings of Al-Anon and the "bad girls" of the Bible to heal the little girl inside of me. Then He used the bruising of my marital relationship with Leather to mold me into a woman that He could use to serve other women and to break the curse of divorce. I will always thank God for Leather.

God uses both blessings and bruising in the lives of all His chosen ones. I am not special in any way. Every day, I fall short of being all that God wants me to be. I have learned not to hesitate when I realize my sin or mistake because I know I can be confident when I sincerely repent. God always administers forgiveness and grace. That is His promise to those who love Him.

In the same way, God wants me to forgive others and administer grace to them. My marriage to Leather was a nineteen-year long opportunity for me to practice forgiving and extending grace. My performance wasn't that great, I promise you. But with God, I was able to make it through. It was an amazingly difficult experience that I would never choose to do over again. I am just being honest. Obedience is always the right answer and curse breaking is no joke!

And just in case I get asked how I treated my third husband at the judgment seat, I will truthfully say, *"I treated him well"*, because *"I can do all things through Christ who strengthens me!!!* God did it!!

I went into my third marriage still driving the car, deciding the turns and the stops and still having wrecks, but I came out resting and relaxing in the back seat. I came out knowing I was *His Girl!!*

It doesn't matter if you know it yet or not. At the perfect time, you will know you are *His Girl too.* It's a process. Remember, He chose you first, but the process is not complete until you chose Him too. Once you do that, you belong to Him. You are *His Girl!!*

Chapter 10

Family Finishes

This chapter on Family Finishes includes a quick final look at my closest family members as they are today. My relationship with God is the most important relationship in my life, but after that comes my relationship with my family members.

I will also share the details of how my visit went with my mother. Remember, I promised to tell you about my visit to see her in Morganton to share the truth of what happened with my father.

Let's begin with my mother. If I could only choose one word to describe my mother it would be *"GRACE"*. Grace is an extravagant gift that only comes from God. I would describe God's grace as un-earned favor or unconditional love.

Grace is a precious gift that is welcomed anywhere and anytime it shows up. To me, my mother was grace personified. My mother was no more perfect than you or I, but she was always there for me, my siblings, her grandchildren, our extended family and for many other people.

While writing in this book about her and my life with her, I came to realize that she administered grace to people throughout her life. She unknowingly had an active and amazing ministry that changed lives. Her ministry did not require a Bible, a church or money. Her unknown ministry was the *ministry of grace*.

I know this to be true because my life was greatly impacted by her ministry of grace. The grace she administered was done quietly and face to face. It was communicated much more by her attitude and actions than by her words. A heart full of unconditional love for people was her secret weapon.

It wasn't until after she had passed that I realized how much her unconditional love for me had cushioned my life. I wonder if she knew the impact her life was having on so many people around her. I don't think that she did, but I will make sure she knows when we meet in heaven.

A young White man she supervised while working at Broughton Hospital shared this story at her Celebration of Life service. He said, "One day on the job he asked her what she would do if her husband came home at 5:30 in the morning, still drunk, wreaking of alcohol and perfume"? He said my mother replied, "I would ask him how

241

he wants his eggs". See, I told you GRACE was an extravagant gift that only comes from God.

I loved her and I knew she loved me. My mother also knew and loved God and His Word. He called her home in 2008 with the four of us circled around her bed declaring our final words of love to her and reading a favorite scripture passage.

I was aware that she was dying. She was in hospice care, but I was not prepared for the void that she left behind. The feeling immediately appeared, like a black hole suddenly appearing in the center of a colorful painting. I have found that my memories of who she was and how she lived have become the perfect fill-in for the black hole.

Today, when I think about my mother, I am still amazed and inspired most by her capacity to love people. She loved all kinds of people and all kinds of people loved her. I think it was because she had this great ability to love unconditionally. She loved you just how you were. She never judged anyone and always showed patience and acceptance to all who came her way. She had a gift for making people feel comfortable in her presence. I loved that about her and how people responded to her. My mother reminded me a lot of my granddaddy and how he treated people.

She understood what God's grace was and choose to be a person who was full of grace. I especially appreciated that quality in her during the many years it took for me to find my way to Jesus Christ. Not once, in all of my messed up adult life and three messed up husbands did my mother ever criticize me or them. She never made me feel ashamed or lose patience with me. Because of who she was and her love for me, we were able to maintain our relationship throughout all the years of my insane, misguided and sinful behavior.

Through it all, she kept my sisters, my brother and I connected by making sure we did things together as a family and always loved including all of her grandchildren. Family was extremely important to her and she made a big deal out of every family event, holiday and special outing.

I always felt that she wanted me to stay close to the family no matter what I was doing behind the scenes. I look back now and feel so grateful for her unconditional love. I thank God and will always be so grateful that He transformed my life in time for her to see me as the daughter she was praying for and as a woman God was using.

When the time came to share the truth of the sexual molestation with my mother, I felt God had prepared me for it. I felt a little anxious because I had no idea what her response would be, but I had already begun to heal emotionally and had grown a little more spiritually. I felt ready to have the talk with my mother. I knew it was the next step in my spiritual growth and in moving forward in ministry. It wasn't easy, but I knew it was necessary for both of us.

The little girl who wanted to be rescued by her mother, but would never risk telling her the truth, had finally been rescued. God sent Jesus, who did it perfectly. Because of His rescue, there was no lingering residue of shattered expectations or left over hurt when I faced my mother. I had found my place of peace and it was time for me to walk in freedom from my past.

I was able to share the truth of the abuse with my mother honestly, confidently and completely. I told her why I was afraid to tell her. She looked shocked, confused and totally overwhelmed. I answered her questions, but I could tell she was not able to process everything she was hearing. Processing it would take time, but she finally knew the truth.

I told her about the meeting I had with my father to confront him with the truth. I told her about his response. I told her I had forgiven him and hoped to build some form of a relationship with him.

She said over and over again how sorry she was that such a thing had happened to me. We confirmed our love for each other. We cried and hugged each other a lot before we parted that day. I felt at peace and relieved now that we had completed that step.

I returned home. I stayed in close contact by calling her often. For a while, she seemed sad and responded angrily at the mention of my father. Knowing she was a woman of faith and dependence on God gave me hope. I knew whatever God was allowing her emotions, mind and heart to go through would work out for her good. After a couple more months she seemed to have worked through it and our lives moved on.

The holidays came and we went home to visit her. My father also came home for a visit. He called to see if he could come by to visit with us at her home. She gracefully said yes. She did not seem to be too pleased about his coming, but she extended him grace. It was the same grace she had extended to me, my siblings and many others over the years. My father came for his visit. He and my mother had an opportunity to talk, but I don't know what was said between them. I did know that I had done what I needed to do even though it took me more than thirty years to do it.

My mother passed it on to us! Her grace is one big piece of her legacy to us. The others pieces are trust in God and love of family. It is hard to beat that combination! Hopefully, my siblings and I are keeping it going and are passing these qualities on to our children and grandchildren.

I didn't realize the full value of my mother influence until after she was gone. Her legacy gains more and more value to me as time passes. Her legacy of extending grace, strong trust in God and love of family has become a guiding star for my siblings and I. Hopefully, I am passing the legacy on to my daughter and to my grandchildren.

Chiffon has been married for more than ten years now. I have chosen the name "Cord" for her husband because of the way he wraps his arms and his life around his family. I thank God every day for Cord and for sending Chiffon a *"real husband"* and for her being able to recognize his qualities. The best way to make up for never having a real husband, is for your daughter to have one. Chiffon is a *"real wife"* to Cord. Together, Cord and Chiffon make a great team.

Cord is a Captain with the City of Atlanta Fire Department and Chiffon works for a large non-profit organization as their Human Resource Manager. Her knowledge as a Licensed Professional Counselor is being utilized everyday with the organization's employees, staff and with the many school age children they serve in the inner-city of Atlanta.

Chiffon and Cord have given me three amazing grandchildren who I have tagged with unique names that I identify with certain Bible characters. I tagged my nine-year old grandson as "Champion", my seven-year old granddaughter as "Star" and my three-year old grandson as "Lion". My grandchildren are blessed to have parents who are living by faith in God and His Word. That blesses me too.

Today, my brother Denim is our family historian. He is the founder of *Save the Family Institute, Inc.*, a non-profit organization that serves families and advocates for family unity. Denim is also the author of six books written on the history of African American descension and resolving the issues of race in America. Denim has two sons and three daughters and still lives here in the Atlanta area.

Today, Lace and her high school sweetheart have been married fifty plus years. That is a huge deal in our family. Between my father, mother, Denim, Satin and myself there have been ten divorces. Out of the four siblings, Lace is the only one who has succeeded in maintaining her first marriage. She gives credit for that to her faith in God and reliance on His Word. After retiring from Western Carolina Center after thirty-years of service, Lace continues to work full-time for an organization that serves mentally disabled people. She works in an administrative position. Lace still lives in Morganton and has one daughter and one son.

Satin retired from being a high school Spanish Teacher after thirty-years of service with the State of North Carolina. She actively serves in her church in several capacities and is involved in on-going service in her community through volunteering. A lot of her time is spent participating in outreach projects to benefit the underserved populations in her community. She is also a source of faith, support, encouragement and love for her many friends. Satin lives in Charlotte, N.C. and has two daughters.

Each of my siblings have stories of their own and there have been both some bitter rain and some sweet rain days in all of our lives. The future is unknown, but we know that we are extremely blessed to have each other, our children, grandchildren and great-grandchildren. I am extremely grateful and thankful to God for my family!

Chapter 11

Who the Heck
is Harold?

You probably noticed the Acknowledgement page and may be wondering who is Harold. *Harold* is the Holy Spirit. *Harold* is the name the Holy Spirit chose for Himself. Now before you tag me as the *"crazy old lady"*, listen to my story. You know I always have one.

Without the participation of the Holy Spirit, there is honestly no way this book would exist. The first reason is that it was never a desire of mine to write a book. It was all God's idea which got transformed into a writing project for me, but it was Harold who kept me in the game until it was completed. It's simple, no Harold, no book!

The only thing I had ever written was papers in college, the curriculum for the missionary academy, my Graduate Project and several Bible Study Lessons for women. Based on my experience with those occasional smaller writing task, I knew writing a book would have to be a monumental undertaking that would require an unknown amount of time and effort. Lastly, I had no idea how to write a book, but I didn't find that out until I had finished the first rendition. Oh well, thank God for Harold!!

I questioned the assignment and then I procrastinated until there was no way to avoid what I was hearing from the Holy Spirit inside me. Finally, I began writing and re-writing almost exactly two years ago. God downloaded the contents of the book to Harold and Harold communicated and walked me through it all. So, at least read on to see how the Holy Spirit became Harold.

It all began after the insurance funds I had from Leather's death were nearly exhausted. I was talking to God about it. I reminded him that I had three marriages, but I never had a real husband. I told Him I needed a husband's provisions and protection, but I did not want a physical husband.

God knew I loved my life just the way it was. I was totally satisfied and content with Jesus doing all the driving and with sharing my life with my family, my friends and with the women I served.

God said, "I will be your husband and my Son Jesus and the Holy Spirit. We will replace the three husbands you never had. We have always been your provider and protector". I knew that was true.

I knew God, Jesus and the Holy Spirit had always been my real source of provision and protection, but hearing this proposal from God made me feel loved and cherished and adored. I was in total and absolute agreement with this proposal. I immediately and joyfully said, "YES" and embraced it. On the inside, I felt as if it was a real-life proposal.

My very next question to God was "Can I have a ring?" The Holy Spirit said, "Yes you can". Then I really got excited!! That day was March 16, 2018. It's in my journal. I sent out emails and text messages shocking my friends with the news. I told them I had gotten married on March 16th but, I did not say who I had married.

They were thinking I had married some mystery man. I kept them hanging on for almost two days. Needless to say, that totally unexpected announcement out of the blue, stirred up a lot of commotion. I had a wonderful time laughing at some of their email responses back to me. They were hilarious. When I told them who my new husbands were, they were SO relieved that they forgot all about the trick I had played on them.

I wrote my vows and I shared my vows with my friends and asked them to keep me accountable. Here are the vows I made to God my Father, Jesus His Son and the Holy Spirit on March 16, 2018:

I root myself in you, I anchor myself in you, I bind myself to you. I submit my will to you. I yield to your ways. I give all of myself over to you. It is my whole heart's desire to please you in everything I do. I will live in this position until I meet you in heaven.

I am sure your question is, "Have you kept them"? I repeat what I said in an earlier chapter, "Every day, I fall short of being all that God wants me to be", but every morning I get back up and try again. Some days, I think I got close to okay until I think back through the day, oh well. But, I keep on trying my best and He keeps on giving me grace and unconditional love. That is what it takes in any marriage. Now back to Harold.

Because of my impending dramatic decrease in income, I had already begun cleaning out my jewelry boxes looking for items that I could live without that could be of some value. I had found a few items and was planning to take them to be cleaned and appraised. I was thinking, it would be perfect if the sale of those old items from my past could fund my ring purchase to begin my new future with my new husbands.

I took them in for cleaning at a mall jewelry store and noticed that the JC Penny Store across from it was advertising a 20% Off jewelry sale. I decided to check it out when I returned to pick them up. After picking them up, I walked across to   JC Penny's and right into their jewelry department.

God said, go look. I said, okay! I already knew what my ring would look like. It would have a narrow silver band that split into two and intertwined on top and it would have a row of small diamonds. I walked up to the counter to begin looking and immediately a sales lady came over to help me.

She was very helpful and she was a woman of faith. In just a few minutes of looking I found it! It was the one! I was thinking, Wow!! The sales lady pulled it out of the case and saw that it had already been marked down 10%. I said, "Wonderful!" She calculated everything including the fitting and taxes, deducted the 20% and it was too much.

I saw that there were a couple other ones just like it in the case so I decided to take a break and see what God was saying. I told her it was beyond what I could spend. I forgot to ask God.

The next day I saw two different reputable appraisers hoping to sell the items I had. I was disappointed by their offers, but I had been warned about what to expect by someone who knew.

I accepted the larger offer and left there thinking, "Lord, what kind of ring can I find for this amount?" The ring I found at JC

Penny's fit my "ideal ring" vision. It was nothing elaborate, but it was perfectly what I wanted.

I decided to go back to JC Penny's and look further thinking I might find another one I liked that cost less. I returned to the store and the same sales lady was there. I saw that as a good sign.

I looked in the case trying not to look at the one I loved. In a few minutes, I found another one that I liked and I ask to see it. It had a more basic traditional style. It was wider and had no intertwining on top. It did have a few small diamonds that were of lesser quality. She pulled it out and it had also been reduced 10%. She ran the figures, deducted the 20% and the cost fit my funds. I did like it okay and it fit the funds I had.

I was about to close the purchase when the sales lady asked me if I had a JC Penny Credit Card. I said no and she said that if I opened an account that day, I could get an additional 20% off the purchase.

I thought, I could get that savings by getting the card, then pay it off using my funds and have nothing owing on the card. While we were waiting for the approval, the sales lady said, do you want to know what the first ring would cost using your Penny's card and I said yes, why not. She ran the figures and the cost was still more than the funds I had.

After finding out that I was approved for the Penny's credit card, I decided to purchase the second ring thinking that I should just be grateful and thankful, especially at that price. The sales lady told me the ring would be sent off for sizing the next morning and it would be about ten days before it would return.

Later that evening, I was talking to God about the situation knowing He knew how I was really feeling inside. He knew the first ring was my heart's desire. So, I asked Him, as my husband, which ring He wanted me to have? I had never asked Him which one He wanted me to have.

"The first one, the one you loved" was His reply. I knew then that He had guided me to the first ring. God said, "you set limits on what I will do for you and you chose the second ring. There are no limits on what I can do for you".

Needless to say, I am wearing the ring I loved right now as I type in these words. If we ever meet, I will show you my ring. Every time I look at it, I feel assured of the love my three husbands have for me.

Learning to listen for God's voice spoken through the Holy Spirit and to watch for what God does by watching the outcomes are two routines that I have acquired that are permanent. (another one is my fitness workouts). I did not make note of when I embraced these routines, but I distinctively remember the occasion when the Holy Spirit's voice became clear and distinctive to me. The experience was so profound that it became my *"most important, priceless "*over the top sweet rain day". Here is how it happened.

255

In 2004, during the viewing of the movie "The Passion of the Christ", I wept along with many others in the theater and watched with great sadness, compassion and love for Jesus as He endured horrendous suffering and the agonizing crucifixion.

As the images on the screen became more graphic the Holy Spirit inside me said "He did that for you…it was done for you". Hearing that, I began to weep more greatly as a full understanding that Jesus sacrificed Himself for me personally, became a real reality. What He did "FOR ME" became real during those moments watching that movie.

Something inside of me changed. The movie was ending, so I began to try to compose myself to leave the theatre. As I turned the corner to go down the ramp the Holy Spirit said, "Now it's YOUR turn. What will you do in response to what Jesus has done for you?"

From my heart, I heard myself say, "You went all the way for me Jesus, I want to go all the way for you". I prayed, "I want to walk in the FULLNESS of Your purpose and plan for my life Lord Jesus". That decision originated from my heart and implanted itself permanently in my heart, not just in my mind. When something gets in my mind it may or may not stick, but when my heart embraces something it sticks.

My whole heart grabbed hold of that decision, wrapped itself around it and has never let it go. It was a decision to do whatever

God said do. Any other plans I had for myself vanished. My heart, mind and my emotions came into agreement. I wanted whatever God wanted. I would do my very best to follow Jesus through the Holy Spirit's guidance from that moment forward.

I felt great peace. I felt excited. I felt content. There was a sense of anticipation and a feeling of being in just the right place. I had gotten in the "back seat". I had submitted my life to walking in the fullness of God's plans and purposes. I am still trying to give it my best shot today. Now, let's get back to Harold.

A few weeks after receiving my ring, I was working out on the steps in the stairwell in my building. I was thinking how good I felt knowing my husbands were taking care of me. I thought, "it would be great if my husbands had a name". I was thinking that the Holy Spirit is the one who is in me and always with me, so I asked the Holy Spirit if He had a name I could call Him. I immediately heard "Harold"! I laughed out loud and said out loud, "Okay! Harold it is! Thank goodness I was alone in that stairwell.

So my three husbands have one name.....Harold! I loved it!! Upon researching the name Harold, I was amazed to find out that the name Harold means power, leader and ruler. All I can say is, *God is amazing!*

I felt like a loved, cherished and adored princess. Only girls really understand the need to feel like this. Will God go that far? Does God really care about such feelings, desires and intimate details? YEP! He absolutely does because He created us. God knows girls thrive on intimacy and intimacy with Him is always available to all of *His Girls*.

Chapter 12

Girl Talk

We have come to the end of our road trip. We began with a girl's road trip and I want to end with another favorite activity that I loved as a girl.

Let's pretend we are pulling back into my driveway and it's twelve midnight. Your car is still parked in front of my house, but you are exhausted and you live twenty-five miles away. Why don't you come on in and stay over-night? Yes, why not?

We can have a Sleep-over!! In my day, we called them Pajama Parties. Do you remember how much fun those were? I am sure girls all over the world have some form of a Sleep-over with girls their age. It is so true, "Girls just wanna have fun!!"

Sleepovers with my best friend Velour are permanent implants in my mind and heart. Velour became my best friend in fourth grade and we remained almost inseparable until I moved to Atlanta and she moved to Greensboro, North Carolina. But, time, distance and different life journeys can never erase the bond that existed between us. That bond is still there with Velour.

Sometimes, Sleepovers are where best friends become best friends. For many girls, a Sleepover with a best friend is the place where dreams are shared and secrets are told. A Sleepover is the perfect place for *Girl Talk.*

It was while sleeping over, that I shared the truth about the molestation with Velour. She was the only person who knew about it during my teen years. Velour was my "ride or die girlfriend" and she will always have a "best friend place" in my heart.

I have already shared all my secrets with you during our road trip. Now, I want to share the details of the two dreams that I have for us as girls.

In early 2003, I was introduced to a very gifted local artist here in Atlanta named Rebecca Johnson. I shared my story and my dream with Rebecca. My story and my plan to reach out and serve a very diverse group of women touched her heart. She painted a rendition of my dream on canvas and presented it to me as a gift to utilize in my ministry to women. The painting is pictured on the opposite page in the center of the collage. The image of Jesus surrounded by the little girls was painted by Rebecca Johnson in 2003. I chose to name the painting *"In His Presence"* after Psalm 16:11. My dream and

261

desire for girls of every age is that they would make Jesus Christ the "centerpiece" of their lives.

The little girls are representative of the little girl inside of every woman. The collage represents my dream of bringing diverse groups of women together and unifying us by our trust, love, and dependence on Jesus Christ. I want to bridge the gap of our differences by utilizing our shared interests and the expected roles and concerns we have in our everyday lives as women. I want to engage us in connecting, supporting and encouraging each other and becoming an example of unity and inclusiveness in this day and time.

The little girl sitting on Jesus's lap is me. Rebecca painted her from my first-grade picture. Rebecca talked her neighbor from across the street into sitting as her model for Jesus. The little African girl sitting on the ground is Chiffon and was painted from a childhood picture. The little Native American Indian girl is a self-portrait of the artist. The other little girls were live models Rebecca chose from her neighborhood and her church.

The dream has not fully materialized yet, but I believe it will. God gave me the vision and the painting, and I have held on to them patiently. I think when the time is just right, my dream will come true. God is still setting it up. You know how He loves set-ups. So, How about you? What is your dream? Are you still believing God for it?

My reasons for wanting these dreams to come true have already been shared in my "Introduction." But, in a few words, I want to do all that I can to contribute to girls of every age, color, and origin having the best lives possible.

In the Introduction, I also mentioned several things in our lives that would fall apart without us girls, like our daily lives, our families, our communities, and probably the world. The reality is that girls are the glue that holds the most important things in our lives together. Here's one more thought....*What would happen if all the women in the world stopped praying?* Yes, I know. Let's not even go there.

One of my dreams is establishing an online and in-person "talk show" for *girls of every age, color, and ethnicity.* I want the talk show to be a place to spotlight our diversity to be an example of unity, harmony, and inclusiveness to the world around us.

I want it to be a place where any girl will feel included, valued, and free to share her story. I want it to be a place where opportunities to *give and receive* help, support, and encouragement are overflowing. I want it to be a place to enjoy being a girl!

I have already created and completed the initial first steps and have named the talk show *"International Girl Talk."* To keep track of my progress with *"International Girl Talk,"* I invite you to visit me at hisgirl.live@gmail.com.

With this book's completion, I will be available for whatever God has next for *"International Girl Talk."* I am anticipating both of my dreams will come true! I can't wait to see what God does next!!

I believe God will bring both dreams to pass because they originated from Him. He is the creator and planter of dreams and visions because He carries out His plans through us. Remember, He finished writing the books of our lives before we had even lived one day. (Psalm 139:16)

Another reason I believe God will do it is that a year ago, He had *Harold* (the Holy Spirit) lead me to my dream church. For the last twenty-four years, my two church congregations have been composed of 99.9% African Americans.

Since 2003, when the painting was finished, I have dreamed of being in a church with a diverse congregation. *Harold* (Holy Spirit) led me to Mountain West Church (MWC) in Tucker, Ga., October 2019. MWC has a uniquely diverse congregation, and people of every age are invited to participate in what God is doing there actively. I often tell people that MWC looks like what heaven is going to look like. At MWC, no one gets left out; that is why it is my dream church!

When I arrived at MWC, I felt led to join the Intercessory Prayer Small Group immediately after arriving. When I went to my first meeting, the first two women I met were a White woman the same age and a younger woman of Puerto Rican descent. They are delightful, and I am delighted and blessed by getting to know them and their families!! I feel perfectly at home at MWC.

My second dream has no limits and holds the potential to impact our world for generations to come. Exciting huh?

Guess what? I am about to begin to live out my role in that dream right here and right now!! My second dream is to share a powerful discovery I made. I want to share this discovery with as many of *His Girls* as possible, and this sleepover (book) is my opportunity and platform to begin doing that. My second dream is starting to come true right now!!

What I discovered changed how I saw myself as a female. It gave me a new perspective on being female and increased my self-value. I found this discovery in the Bible. You may have discovered it too. I hope you have and that you are already applying this knowledge to your life as a female, but just in case, here is how it happened and what I discovered.

I discovered it years ago from the very first "bad girl" in the Bible. This "bad girl" also happens to be our "Original First Lady." I am talking about Eve, and of course, it all begins in the Garden of Eden.

As someone with a never-ending passion for helping women, I have searched for answers, insights, and wisdom from most women in the Bible. Being the first woman and being created by God's own hands made Eve's behavior of extra-special interest to me. (see Genesis 2: 16- 3: 24)

There is an enormous amount of insight that girls can glean from this "bad girls'" life. Just like my life story, a girl can also learn what not to do from Eve's story. Those "what not to do" lessons can be precious too.

For instance, Eve was enticed by the serpent, who said the fruit would give her knowledge that would make her like God. She was attracted by the fruit looking good to eat, by it being pleasant to look at, and by the idea that it would make her wise.

As girls today, we are still falling prey to wanting to be the smartest and the wisest. We are always tempted by food and by wanting pretty things, sometimes to the point of our detriment. Everything began in the garden, and in my opinion, not much has changed, including the serpent (satan). He is still a liar and a deceiver who sets traps for us.

After reading the Genesis account many times in the Bible, I had many questions about Eve's role as the female counterpart to Adam. My first question was, "Why was Eve talking to a serpent?" Really Eve?

Another question was, "Why did the serpent go to Eve instead of Adam?" I also had a big "what if" question about Eve's disobedient response. "What if she had said "no thank you" when offered the fruit and kept it moving. If she had turned and walked away, what do you think Adam would have done?

The Genesis account says that when the serpent offered the fruit, both Eve and Adam were present. Genesis 2: 6 says, "Eve took the fruit and did eat and gave it also to her husband with her, and he did eat." The outcome of their choices had an eternal significance that has to be dealt with by every human being created since that moment.

But, I do not want us to focus on the eternal significance of how Eve's choice affected our lives. I want us to focus on the importance of how Eve's choice affected Adam.

I believe Adam's decision to eat the fruit was influenced by Eve's decision to eat the fruit. I think the serpent approached Eve first because he was aware of *"Eve's influence."* I believe the serpent already knew that once he won Eve over, Adam would follow.

The serpent's cunning approach utilizing the woman's influence has been used throughout time since then. I had seen this kind of interaction before. As a child back in my neighborhood, some door-to-door salesmen came by our homes during the day. They never came in the evening when our fathers were at home. It was always during the day when only our mothers were at home. One sold encyclopedia's, one sold vacuum cleaners, one sold insurance, and one sold bed linens and bedspreads out of the trunk of his car, but they all came during the day.

267

These salesmen knew the secret of the wife's influence. The salesmen knew that once the wife made up her mind that she wanted something that he was selling, most often, it would only be a matter of time before she used her influence to convince her husband to go along with the purchase.

Eve found the fruit appealing in several ways and decided she wanted to eat it and then offered it to Adam, who also ate it. God, Himself, had told Adam not to eat of that tree, and Adam told Eve what God had said. Yet, when Eve ate, Adam ate. It was Eve's influence that affected Adam.

Our influence, like a two-sided coin, is either for doing good or for doing bad. Even without speaking, our impact can still be felt and is either promoting what is excellent or bad.

Knowing what I know about the male and female relationship, I believe if Eve had turned and walked away, Adam would have too. If Eve had said, "Remember what God said, Adam," it would have been more than enough to stop this train wreck.

Before God created Eve, He gave Adam the direct command to not eat of the tree. It was a clear act of disobedience that God would first hold Adam accountable for, but He would also confront Eve for her disobedience.

Before eating the fruit, God had given them dominion over the earth together. After their disobedience, God cursed Eve with painful childbirth and issued Adam's rule over her.

In Genesis 3: 17, God pronounces the curses over Adam's life. This is what God says to Adam in that verse, *"because you listened to your wife* and ate fruit from the tree, which I commanded you not to eat from, cursed is the ground because of you,"* and then God goes on to pronounce the curses.

God gave Adam rule over Eve. Adam was offered the position of headship over Eve. But, Eve still could *influence.* God did not take away Eve's ability to influence Adam.

Eve's problem was that she was using her influence for selfish gain and not for good. Her impact caused disobedience to God's command and resulted in the entry of sin into the world.

Influence is power!! The power of influence is the discovery I made from Eve. As females, we all have an impact!! Think about it. You and I can influence the people around us towards good choices or bad choices, just like Eve.

Influence is so powerful that it can work without saying a word. It can be communicated by our actions and attitudes just as well as our words. Often, it works more effectively through actions and without words.

My second dream is coming true right now!! I am sharing my discovery with you now!! God has given *His Girls* the ability to be a positive influence in our little corners of the world, and that is something that we can all do. If each one of us does that, each little corner will get brighter. Corner by corner, the world will gradually keep getting brighter and brighter. Wouldn't it be wonderful to make God smile when He sees our little lights all over the world getting brighter?

God has entrusted us with being the glue that holds the essential things in our lives and the world together. Each of us can positively impact the men in our lives by our positive examples, whether those men are our husbands, fathers, brothers, grandfathers, uncles, or cousins. The future can be brighter for our children, grandchildren, great-grandchildren, nieces, nephews, a younger sister or brother, or any family member in the younger generations. We can choose to positively influence all of their lives through our obedience to God and His Word.

Influence your family towards God's ways, and the world will get brighter and brighter. Let's use our influence to make our little corner of the world a more peaceful, kinder, safer, and more harmonious environment for the next generation.

Based on our track record for holding things together, I believe a combined effort by all *His Girls* could significantly impact our world today.

Thank you for taking the road trip with me. Thank you for staying for the Sleep Over and allowing me to share my dreams with you.

A new day has dawned, and it's time for you to hop in your car and return to your everyday life. But before you depart, I have one last thing to share with you that girls love. It's a "take-away-bag" full of things every girl needs, and they all come from the heart of a senior-age girl who cares and *"who has been there and done that."* I have the ball cap, the t-shirt, the tote bag, and the water bottle to prove it!!

My most significant and most urgent desire is that you take a relationship with Jesus Christ with you. If you already came with that relationship intact, that's even better. If you have been thinking about taking the step since you read my "surrender to Jesus as Savior story" in Chapter Seven, then let's make your "U-turn" right now.

Admit that you have sinned and ask God to forgive you of your sins. Tell God that you believe that Jesus is His son and ask Jesus to come into your heart and be your Savior and Lord. That's it! CONGRATULATIONS!! You are saved!!. You are now *His Girl!!!*

Contact someone you know who is a surrendered believer in Jesus Christ and give them your good news. Get a Bible and begin reading in John's book to understand who Jesus is and start your relationship with Him. Find a Bible-centered church to attend or view online. Seek out friends who are saved believers and connect with them. Read Ps. 139: 1-18 to understand who God is and how He relates intimately to you.

I believe Jesus has chosen every girl who reads this book. As I said in the Introduction, "Even if you have not chosen Him yet or feel you never will, He has plans to win you over. If He has chosen you, it's just a matter of time. Whether you are six-years-old or one-hundred and six-years-old when you choose Him, you will be *His Girl* forever once you do. Now let's look at some of the other items I tucked into your "take away bag".

What I have written in this book is for every woman and girl who does not know her value or has been told through words or actions that she is not valuable. I hope this book reaches the hands of women who do not know their identity and those who are trapped by their self-doubt, shame, or guilt.

I hope it reaches teenage girls and young women searching for love in all the wrong places at this very moment. I hope it gets the hurting little girls buried inside of adult women who are in deep denial and those who are secretly suffering from acts that long ago stripped away their self-value, identity, and dignity. I know your pain. I lived in it for thirty-two years of my life, and I say to all of you, "I know what it feels like, but I also know there is so much more for you."

I know your value and worth. I know your identity. You belong to God! You are loved! You are cherished! You are not forgotten! You have a purpose! You have a destiny and a future! You matter! You are IMPORTANT!

There is a unique God-designed purpose and plan just for you. Attaining it will require belief in God and His Word, a trusting relationship with Him through Jesus and the Holy Spirit, and the ability to wait. God loves you. There is grace for you, just like there was for me. You are never outside of God's reach. His arms reach out for you long and wide, just like they did for me. "You Are His Girl!!!" Just like me, You belong to God!!!

This is how being *His Girl* has affected my life and how it can affect yours too. God loves us, no matter what!! With Him, my past did not matter. He already knew every detail even before it happened. I can be "me" all the time with Him. Even on my worst day, God still loves me. I can look like "me" even at seventy-two and still feel beautiful! I can tell Him how I feel, mess up, make bad choices, and never be condemned by God. When I fail, His love never fails me.

When God convicts me, I repent, and along with my repentance comes another chance to get it right. I always feel safe with Him. His love for me will never change and will last eternally, no matter what I do. All these characteristics about God have made me love

Him more and more, and my desire to please Him grows as He continues to love me unconditionally.

.I wanted to give you the "inside scoop" on my thirty-plus-year love story with Jesus Christ because I want you to have everything I have. I had no idea He loved me as He does. I had no idea of what His love was capable of doing in my messed-up, issue filled life, but now I know, and I want you to know. I hope that your hearts desires are fulfilled but I want you to know that having an earthly man, riches, youth, beauty, fame, or power is not necessary for genuine and authentic success-- not at all.

I have none of these things. What I have is of far greater value. What I have received is priceless. I know who I am, I know my purpose for being here on earth, and I love being me! Because I am His Girl, I am aware that I am walking in my destiny and purpose.

Every day, I am seeking the fullness of HIS purpose and plan for my life. This is my most passionate desire for every *girl*.....that she would know how much she is loved and walk in the fullness of God's purpose and plan for her life too and fall in love with God and become *His Girl!!* That is high end living!!

Because I am His Girl, I know my steps are pre-ordered by God. I am where I should be, whole, satisfied, and content. I love being me!! This is my life in Him when I stay tuned in, and my focus is on Him.

However, I do sometimes get distracted, make mistakes, and fall short. I am still a real person with real-life happening. I have moments or times where my mind, feelings, and emotions get me caught up in the world around me and draw me away from Him, but that never changes who God is or what He will do to take care of me. I am not perfect, but He is.

What I am saying is that as soon as I can get my eyes focused back on Him, get a grip on my emotions and refocus myself on His Word, I start coming back to where I need and want to be in Him. I always find Him there, waiting for me.

I am "an everyday girl," for sure. I am a seventy-two-year-old widow, living in a senior community, who looks forward to her funds arriving on the 3rd day of each month. I have no money, fame, power, youth, beauty, or special abilities. My highest paying job ever only earned me about $36,000 annually. I am well off, influential, useful, fulfilled, content, and still feel young and beautiful on the inside because I belong to Him.

But so much more than all of this, belonging to Him gives me the best life I can have. It allows me to be used by Him. This is where a successful life and genuine fulfillment get defined. Living my life in the predestined purposes and plans of God is living over the top! That is what I decided to aim for and how I am finding the quality of my life at seventy-two going up, up, up!!

During the years I spent doing all the driving, I made many wrong turns, harmful stops, and had numerous wrecks. Despite all this, God has healed me from the agony and torment of years of childhood molestation at the hand of my father. Because of my relationship with God, I could forgive my father and reconnect with him a few years before his death.

Because of my relationship with God, I see "the good things" I inherited from my father despite what happened. I see my father's imprint on my life in my love of nature and the outdoors, my love of sports and fitness, and even in my sense of humor. All things do work together for good!!

God has forgiven, delivered, and restored me from years of sexual immorality, including adultery, delivered me from a mindset of "people-pleasing" and from a lifestyle of using drugs and alcohol. God has healed and restored me from multiple divorces and has broken the curse of divorce in my life.

My brokenness, the spiritual, mental, emotional damage and the damage from my bad choices have all been repaired. I have a new identity, and I see my value and worth. I thank God that at forty-two years old, it was not too late for me.

Let me make it clear, I victoriously survived all of this not because of anything I did, but because of what God and Jesus did for me.

God turned my bitter rain days into sweet rain by using my bitter rain days to give other women hope. Inside my greatest pain was where I found my greatest purpose. Only God could do that!!

What I say about God, Jesus, and the Holy Spirit is based on what I have seen happen in my life. The evidence I see in my own life confirms and matches what the Bible says. My faith and belief in God, Jesus, and the Holy Spirit increases as my relationship grows more in-depth with them. When I look at the outcomes, my love for God grows, and I hold on tighter to Him.

If you aren't His Girl, you can be. I promise you that He wants you to be His Girl too!! I promise you that your life will get better as you go deeper in Him. If you do, one day you will want to write your *"Love Story"* about God too.

These are the outcomes I have experienced. The evidence is clear to me, and it keeps piling up. I have made my decision. I will be a witness for God, Jesus, and the Holy Spirit because I was at the scene of the wreck. I saw everything. I was the wreck! NOW, I AM *HIS GIRL!*

Here are a few Bible Scriptures that can help you get to know God, Jesus and the Holy Spirit more intimately.

Psalms 139: 1-18

The Book of John

John 15: 16

Contact me at: hisgirl.live@gmail.com

Made in the USA
Columbia, SC
14 January 2022